Alone It Stands

A play

John Breen

Samuel French — London
New York - Toronto - Hollywood

Please see page iv for further copyright information.

ALONE IT STANDS

First presented at Waterpark Rugby Club on 15th
September 1999 with the following cast:

Malcolm Adams
Conor Delaney
Gerry McCann
Ciaran McMahon
Niamh McGrath
Karl Quinn

Directed by John Breen
Lighting by Gerard Meagher

Subsequently presented by Pat Moylan and Breda Cashe
for Lane Productions Ltd at the Duchess Theatre, London,
on 3rd January 2002 with the following cast:

Malcolm Adams
Dessie Gallagher
Garrett Lombard
Gerry McCann
Niamh McGrath
Paul Meade

Directed by John Breen
Decor by Jack Kirwan
Lighting by James C McFetridge

CHARACTERS

FIRST ACTOR

Gerry, Munster fan
Seamus Dennisson, Munster player
Dan Canniffe, Donal Canniffe's father
BJ Robertson, All Black player
Bridie Walsh, barmaid
Irene, posh Cork supporter
Bunratty Singer
Priest

SECOND ACTOR

Lanky, Munster fan
Donal Canniffe, Munster player
BBC Commentator
Rodney, posh Cork supporter
Johnstone, All Black player
Bunratty Singer
Williams, All Black player
Nurse
Dunn, All Black player

THIRD ACTOR

Tony Ward, Munster player
Russ Thomas, All Black player
Ashworth, All Black player
David, posh Cork supporter
Monica, child
Jasper, child
Bunratty Singer
Brendan Foley, Munster player
Wayne Graham, All Black player
Dan's Friend 1
Donaldson, All Black player

FOURTH ACTOR

Spider, child
Fox O' Halloran, President of Shannon Rugby Club
Tom Kiernan, Munster coach
Andy Haden, All Black player
Graham Mourie, All Black player
Relative at Funeral
"Locky", Gerry McLoughlin, Munster player
Dan's friend 2
Spectator

FIFTH ACTOR

Stu Wilson, All Black player
Ferret, child
Dog (Sinbad)
Bunratty Singer
Pat Whelan, Munster player
Jim Bowen, Munster player
All Black Fan 1
Taxi Driver
Nurse
Bottom of Tall NZ fan
Tucker, Munster player
Greg Barrett, Munster player
All Black Forward

ACTRESS

Mary, Gerry's wife
Dandy, child
Moss Keane, Munster player
Marjorie, posh Cork supporter
Bunratty Singer
Gary Knight, Munster player
Top of big NZ fan
Ball
McKechnie, All Black player

AUTHOR'S NOTES

Setting

The play was originally performed with a 16 foot by 12 foot rectangle of black judo mats taped together on the floor with a thick strip of white tape aound the edges to clearly mark the playing space. There were two benches either side of the stage; the actors sat on these when not performing. The actors were visible to the audience at all times. There were water bottles at the side of the stage so that the actors could re-hydrate between scenes. Later productions added a scenic skyscape of Limerick city.

It is open to the director and designer to use whatever set they wish, but I would recommend the mats as they enable a very physical production.

Costume

The six actors wear the 1978 versions of All Black gear in Act I and Munster gear in Act II. The All Black kit consists of a plain black jersey with a white collar and a white fern embroidered over the heart; black shorts and black socks. The Munster kit is: a plain crimson red jersey with a white collar and long sleeves and a badge showing three gold crowns on a black background with gold edging; white shorts and red socks.

Performance style

As there are no costume changes, it is up to the actors to create the various characters they play using their bodies and voices. My most constant note to actors over the years has been to "trust the story" — don't try to *make* it funny, it is funny.

John Breen

THE HAKA: PRONUNCIATION

Ka Maa Tay Ka Maa Tay Cow Ra Cow Ra
Ka Maa Tay Ka Maa Tay Cow Ra Cow Ra
Ten Nay Tay Tang Ga Ta Poo Roo Hoo Roo
Nah Mah E Tee Kee My Fa Ka Feet Ti Tay Rah
Ooh Pa Nay Ooh Pa Nay
Ohh Pa Nay Kuu Pa Nay
Feet Ti Tay Rah
Heeee!

ACT I
SCENE 1

The front of the stage floor is covered by judo mats taped together. There are two benches, R and L, on which the actors sit when "off" (no-one ever leaves the stage)

When the play begins the stage is in darkness

Drums

The actors enter and stand in Haka formation at the back of the stage behind the mats

Lights come up, backlighting the actors from floor level

All (*whispering; for pronunciation see facing page*)
> Ka mate, ka mate, ka ora, ka ora,
> Ka mate, ka mate, ka ora , ka ora.
> Tenei te tangata puhuruhuru,
> Nana i tiki mai whaka whiti te ra.
> Up ane upane,
> Up ane kaupane,
> Whiti te ra.

Stu Wilson jumps forward C, turning as he jumps so that he lands facing US. A spot comes up C

Wilson My ball.

The actor playing Gerry attacks Wilson but is shouldered off. The Lights come up full on the whole stage

The actress attacks Wilson and is palmed off. The actors playing Tony Ward and Lanky go high and low and are thrown off. Finally the actor playing Spider charges and is judo-thrown on to the mats

The actor playing Lanky gets up and speaks as a BBC commentator

BBC Commentator The twenty-fifth of October 1978. Wilson and the All Blacks have demolished this Cardiff side. They'll be crying in the valleys of Glenethlie tonight.

All but Wilson groan. The Lights change to a cold night-time exterior state

All but Wilson and the actress sit on the benches. The actor playing Wilson growls at them as they go

SCENE 2

Wilson goes on all fours facing UL; *the actress goes on all fours toe to toe with him so that, together, they form a car*

Ward and Fox O'Halloran come forward. Ward stands to one side of the car and Fox mimes putting a fuel nozzle into the tank

Fox Do you want me to check the oil?
Ward No, you're grand, just fill her up.
Fox I suppose you're headed for Fermoy?
Ward I am, yeah.
Fox That must be a bit of a pain in the hole.
Ward It is, yeah.
Fox Athlone would have made more sense. What good is Fermoy to anyone?
Ward Sort of a neutral venue for training.
Fox I suppose you have it there. (*He replaces the nozzle in its holder and moves* C)

Ward follows Fox and pays him during the following

Well, you're all set there so, that'll be two pounds seventy-five. I'd say ye'll have some crowd at the game in a fortnight. They have me tormented lookin' for tickets. Some of the Shannon lads were telling me Tom Kiernan is putting ye through hoops below in Fermoy.
Ward Oh, he is that. I'm sorry, Fox, I'm in a hurry but — ah — I'll see you at the game. (*He makes to get into the car*)
Fox Are you nervous at all, Tony?
Ward Ah, it'll be a tough game but they're only human, same as ourselves.
Fox There's a fair bit more humanity to them, all the same, though, Tony. I've never seen a team as big. The crowd that were over in '74 were big, but these lads are enormous. Did you see the game against Cardiff?
Ward No, I prefer not to see the opposition.

Fox They hammered them into the ground! Tackle them early, Tony, and take your chances, that's my advice — if they get running at all, ye can kiss yer arses goodbye. Say hallo to Tom Kiernan for me.

Ward Right, I will. (*He gets into the car*)

Fox And Tony ... (*He knocks on the window of the car*)

Ward winds down the window, the action accompanied by a sound effect from one of the car actors

Bite, boot and bollock.

The Lights snap to a bright daytime exterior state

Fox, Ward and the car actors return to the benches

SCENE 3

Gerry MacNamara and his friend Lanky come DS

Gerry and Lanky are in a queue. As the scene progresses they shuffle from L *to* R, *as the queue moves*

Lanky You're havin' me on.

Gerry I wish I was. But she has her heart set on it and I'm boxed into a corner.

Lanky Sur' can't you just say no?

Gerry How can I? Any time I open my mouth about it she gives me chapter and verse. I said I wanted to support her — well, this is where it starts.

Lanky Standing around like a spare prick while she has a baby?

Gerry Bees.

Lanky What?

Gerry Ba*bies*. She's having twins.

Lanky Whatever !

Gerry It's not like that, Lanky; I can help her with the breathing and stuff. Her cousin's a midwife over in London and all the fathers are present at the birth — it's no big deal.

Lanky Jesus, Gerry. The slaggin' you'd get !

Gerry That's just it, Mary says I'm more afraid of what the lads'll say than anything else.

Lanky It's just not natural, Gerry. (*Into an imaginary ticket booth*) Two tickets please — terrace.

There is an awkward pause

So do you think Locky and Brendan Foley have their place for the game?

Gerry Sur' who else is there? It's all politics anyway.

Lanky Gerry, don't start.

Gerry (*with mounting indignation*) Look at the team: four from Garryowen, two from Cork Con, two from UCC, Canniffe a Corkman from Landsdowne Spring, a Kerryman from Trinity, one from London, and Shannon only gets three players. It's a conspiracy.

Lanky Give it a rest.

Gerry I will not give it a rest. It's not about the best players, it's horse trading. A bunch of wankers in sheepskin jackets passing around brandy and cigars in Montenotty deciding who'll play the best team in the world? Sur' what chance do we have?

Lanky Did you have any luck with that job?

Gerry That's more of it. Didn't Mungo Johnny get in ahead of me on Friday? His cousin heard about it in South's on Wednesday night. And what rugby club does Mungo's cousin play with?

Together Garry — feckin' — owen.

Gerry That club is the bane of my life. Every turn I take Garryowen are there waitin' for me. They've every job in the town sewn up.

Lanky Wasn't Mary's da a great Garryowen man in his day?

Gerry Mary's da is an honest working man, a plumber. And like all honest working Limerick men he played rugby for Shannon. Mary's da only ever visited Garryowen Rugby Club once, seven years ago, to fix the showers, and they still haven't paid him. What's keepin' your one with the tickets?

Lanky has some words with the (invisible) ticket agent

Lanky (*whispering to Gerry*) They've no feckin' tickets left.

Gerry That's more of it. I'm telling you if we have to go to Garryowen to get tickets no good will come of it. It'll put a hex on the whole thing. We'd be as well staying at home and giving them some chance.

Lanky Will you stop with your rawmeish.

Gerry I'm tellin' you, every turn I make.

The Lights change to a night-time exterior setting

Lanky returns to the benches

SCENE 4

The training ground in Fermoy

Gerry becomes Seamus Dennison and mimes doing squats under a barbell

Tom Kiernan, the coach, comes DS and watches Seamus

Kiernan (*to Seamus*) When you are an athlete in peak condition it doesn't take a lot of work to maintain that. But to break through your own personal plateau and reach an altered state of fitness, where your body is so attuned that even your perceptions are sharper, one must have qualities that are rare even among athletes. It's all about pain, Seamus, about accepting excruciating pain as part of the fabric of your everyday life. Your body doesn't feel safe working this hard. It sends out signals to this effect. Your lungs ache, legs feel tired and heavy, your head feels tight, mouth dry. You ignore it, accept it. Now your body gets more persistent. Stop. Pain. Stop. Pain. Stop. This is when most people do stop. But if you look at great athletes in their prime, at the final stretch of the fifteen hundred metres at the Olympics, if you look at the faces of the runners as they come down that final straight, or at the face of a wing forward making a break for the line late in an International — the look on their faces isn't elation, Seamus, it's agony.

Tom Kiernan returns to the benches shaking his head

Seamus (*to the audience*) When we arrive in Fermoy we go to the Grand Hotel and get into our togs. Then we travel in a selection of motorcars to the army field outside the town. We have to line the cars up along the touchline with the engines running and the lights on so we can see what we're doing. The grass is eight inches long. There are nettles and dock leaves. Tom Kiernan has us training like he hates us.

Ward comes DS as though slowing down after a sprint. He has been training too

Seamus and Tony train together (star jumps or burpees) during the following

Seamus (*to Ward*) How's Dublin treating you, Wardy?
Ward   Not too bad, Seamus.
Seamus It must be grand to be home all the same. I'd say Limerick seems mighty quiet after a place like Dublin.
Ward   Ah, you'd miss Limerick all the same, though.
Seamus Oh? I thought you'd only be too glad to be out of the place.
Ward   Ah no, God no. I'll tell you rugby is a different game altogether in Limerick
Seamus How do you mean?

Tony stops exercising. Seamus continues

Ward Well, I was driving down here last week for training. I had to pass through Limerick. I dropped in to get petrol out by the Regional Hospital. And the guy that filled up my tank was the President of Shannon Rugby Club.

Seamus stops what he's doing

Seamus Fox O'Halloran.
Ward Exactly.
Seamus Yeah?

Seamus doesn't get it

Well, the idea that a man like Fox O'Halloran, from Ballynanty with a regular job like that could become President of a big Dublin club, say Landsdowne or Wanderers. They wouldn't let it happen, Seamus. Rugby is a religion in Limerick. You've grown up with it, so you don't notice it. When I got the shout for Garryowen, well the whole next week people kept coming up to me, asking me how we'd do next Saturday. Little old ladies at bus stops showing me how to tackle. People all over the city saluting me like one of their own. It was like being in a big family. And then we beat Shannon.
Seamus Oh, hoo, yes.
Ward Then the town became schizophrenic. Love on one side and, well, not hate but certainly abuse on the other.
Seamus Kick the film star.
Ward That was the least of it. I miss it though. It was great crack.

Tom Kiernan comes DS

Kiernan Seamus, a word.

Seamus looks at Tony. He knows what's coming. Then he moves away

Ward becomes Jasper, Kiernan becomes Spider; two kids. Dandy and Ferret move to them

They introduce themselves

Spider Spider.

The Lights snap to a bright daytime exterior setting

Jasper Jasper.

Dandy Dandy.
Ferret Ferret.
Spider Right what have we got. Dandy?
Dandy Eight cardboard boxes, some damp chipboard, a load of ivy, wallpaper from the scary house, old banisters, three tins of paint, two dried-up Christmas trees, box hedging from the backs, two car seats, half a tree, and I know where there's a skip.
Spider Ferret?
Ferret Four firelighters.
Spider Right. I know where there's a load of carpet and lino.
Jasper Carpet?
Spider Burns great! Did you bring the hatchet?
Dandy Couldn't find it. I brought me da's Swiss army knife. We can't use it but ——
Jasper Why not?
Dandy If he finds out I robbed it he'll kill me.
Spider We need a hatchet.
Ferret Cossie's da has one; we could ask him.
Spider Nah.
Dandy Why not ?
Spider He's working for the O'Mahonys.
Dandy Bastard.
Ferret I met him goin' up the backs with two chairs. He said the O'Mahony's da was buyin' loads of crisps an' everythin' for the bonfire.

Spider gives Ferret a dirty look

He has a hidin' comin', that young fellah.
Dandy Their da has a trailer an' ever'thin'. Works down the docks.
Jasper Yeah, along wit your mudder!

Jasper and Dandy tussle briefly. Spider breaks up the fight

Spider I don't care if their da owns Bord na Mona. We have to have a bigger bonfire than them. Pat O'Mahony made a mock of me yesterday.
Jasper Did you clock him? What did he say?
Spider He said no-one would come to our jammy bonfire when they could get crisps an' lemonade floats over in their place. He said any one workin' with us couldn't play football in their back garden.
Jasper Lousers.
Spider He said his little sister Monica saw us robbin' apples an' their ma said if she saw us round the place she'd call the Guards.
Ferret Monica O'Mahony is a real squealer.

Jasper Yeah, she got Tommy Hartnett thrown out of the Gaeltacht for speaking English.

Dandy Yeah, and she got me thrown out of the bell ringers!

Ferret Why ?

Dandy I couldn't reach the ropes.

Spider She's trouble. She thinks she's right posh just 'cause she does a bit of horse-ridin' out in Patrickswell. If you look at her crooked she calls her ma. Anyone caught talkin' to Monica is out of the gang, agreed ?

All Agreed!

Spider Ye know what we're missing, don't ye?

Ferret What?

Spider Tyres. Adds volume, you get a great quality of flame and thick black smoke.

The others are inspired

Ferret Where are we going to get tyres?

Spider I know a place we can get them on Tuesday.

Dandy I can't on Tuesday; my da is takin' me to the match.

Spider You're going to a match on the most important day of the year?

Dandy Well, me da has the tickets bought.

Spider You won't see the O'Mahonys going to a match, will you? No, they'll be working. They have their priorities right. But you go lickin' up to your da. Think about it, Dandy; it's only a poxy rugby match. Easily forgotten. But this bonfire will live in your memory forever. When people ask you "Did you build this? Were you part of this?" are you going to say "No, I was at a rugby match." Have you no shame?

Dandy I don't want to go but me da has his heart set on it.

Spider (*looking at Ferret*) Have you any smokes?

Ferret Consulate.

Spider is unimpressed

Jasper (*proudly*) Major.

Spider takes a Major from Jasper. Spider, Ferret and Jasper consult noisily

Spider If you don't want to pal around with us we'll understand.

They pull on their cigarettes and blow smoke at Dandy

The O'Mahonys are always looking for people.

Spider leaves, followed by Ferret and Jasper; they make faces at Dandy as they go. Dandy is devastated and moves off in the opposite direction

Scene 6

The All Blacks — including Wilson, BJ Robertson and Graham Mourie — come forward

Wilson and Robertson move DC; the others train. Their pace is more languid than that of the Munster players

Robertson Yeah.

The Lights snap to a night-time exterior setting with white floodlights

They have this medieval castle outside Limerick where the Bunratty Singers perform — hell, babes that can really sing — and this stuff called mead...

Wilson Mead ?

Robertson Yeah, it's like a drink made from honey. So the girls are singing away, you're eating your food with your bare hands, and your head is spinning from this lethal booze, I'm telling you bros it's a great night out. Last time we were here the girls were all over us. I think Limerick women see the game of rugby as more of a mating ritual than a sport.

Wilson Yeah, but Russ isn't going to let us near the place, is he?

Robertson He might. It's only Munster on Tuesday and they haven't been playing that well. I think if a few of us asked for a night off he'd be game.

Wilson Rather you than me, mate.

Russ enters

Russ What the fuck do you two think you're doing ?

Wilson We're just warming, boss.

Russ Bollocks, you should have been warmed up a half an hour ago. I said fifteen hundred press-ups before ball work and I meant it.

Robertson sighs

All right, Wilson, that's an eighty dollar fine.

Wilson What for ?

Russ Audible sighing. I won't stand for that. You lot are walking around like film stars; posing for photographs, autographing sweaters.

Robertson You told us to win hearts and minds, boss.

Russ Don't split hairs with me, boy. Complacency is our enemy, boys. Now I keep hearing about training runs against regional teams before the main event? (*To Mourie*) That is not what the All Blacks are about. You consider yourselves as the pinnacle of rugby talent. You're here to give the locals a lesson in how it should be played. Chase a few girls, have a few beers, a nice easy run against a bunch of local yahoos, all very nice and friendly. You know what these local yahoos see when they look at you? (*Pause*) Anyone? (*Pause*) They see the most desirable virgin in all of rugby. Pure. Unsullied by defeat. And they want you. Look at how we're pissing about! You know what happens to virgins who piss about ?

Wilson No.

Russ They get fucked! If you girls don't wake up and rediscover your pride and dignity that's what Munster will do to you. (*To Robertson*) They nearly beat us in '74, yeah ? Do you want to go home and say "We lost. They beat us. We let them."?

Robertson No.

Russ No. We travelled around the world to get beaten by a bunch of scrawny Irish peasants? Now they think we're arrogant. Because we are the best. And they hate us. They want to grind our noses in defeat. Now, they will tackle like demons, they will ruck and scrum like wild animals. They're fast and unpredictable. (*Beat*) But they're small. If we don't let them have the ball they can't score. We control the game up front. No fancy stuff. A good hard clinical performance, and we will hammer these poor bastards. And, Wilson, any more talk of mead or Bunratty women ——

Wilson But, Boss ...

Russ — and I swear I will personally deflower you myself.

The white floodlights snap off

All the All Blacks apart from Mourie and the actor about to play Donal Canniffe return to the benches

SCENE 7

We're back in Fermoy

Mourie becomes Tom Kiernan. Donal Canniffe joins him

During the following, Seamus comes DS and overhears the conversation

Canniffe This is ridiculous Tom, Seamus Dennison has to play. He has experience against them in the past; he's fast; he's the best tackler in the team.

Kiernan Granted, but he's only eleven stone. The lightest player the All Blacks have is nearly thirteen stone.

Canniffe But Tom ——

Kiernan We can't afford to let them through the centre. Every time they break through our first line of defence it'll cost us six points. There's no decision made yet, Donal, I thought it was only fair to warn him. It was a private conversation, Donal, you had no right to be listening in.

Seamus They won't get by me, Tom, two stone or no two stone. The one part of my game I've always been sure of is my tackling. If your hands are tied then fair enough, you're the boss, but I've never been fitter or sharper. And I'll tackle any man, on any part of the pitch. He'll go down and I'll get up before him, first back into play, no matter who I hit.

The floodlights snap on again

The cast become the All Blacks

SCENE 8

We're back in the All Blacks camp

Tom Kiernan becomes Mourie; Wilson and Russ Thomas join him

Wilson What about Tony Ward?

Russ Tony Ward is their problem

Mourie I've seen him play, boss, he's a match winner. You never know what he's going to do.

Russ Exactly, and neither do his own centre halfs. Every time he gets the ball he does something different — little jinky runs — they never know where he's going. His unpredictability is their weakness.

Mourie Well, Tony Ward has a great boot on him; if we give away soft penalties, he'll punish us. He can drop a goal from anywhere inside our half.

Russ Not if we don't let them have the ball. If we rush him every time he gets the ball to hand, punish him for his little jinky runs, two-man tackles high and low, he'll start to make erratic decisions. Then their gameplan is gone. We have to smash through the centre, good clean ball to the backs, hammer our way through. They won't be able to hold us out for eighty minutes if we are fit and focused. Now we are here to honour our country. (*Beat*) So there'll be no more talk of pubs or women till after the game on Tuesday.

The Lights change to an interior setting

The cast become the Munster players

SCENE 9

Back in Fermoy

Russ Thomas becomes Ward; Mourie becomes Tom Kiernan

Kiernan (*to Ward*) Tony, your job is to keep them guessing — little jinky runs, they won't know where you're going. Your unpredictability is one of our strengths. We've got to break their momentum, keep them going backwards. Put little balls over the defence for our lads to run on to. Do what you do best. We're used to your little ways. Keep them guessing, get the ball back in front of our forwards when you can, and if you think something's on, have a go. I'm not going to talk about their tactics, we'll focus on what we do when we have the ball. When they have it the tactics are simple: put them down, make the first tackle count.

The Lights change to a cold interior setting

Tom Kiernan and Ward return to the benches

SCENE 10

Mary, heavily pregnant, comes forward. An actor becomes a chair for her C; she sits. Gerry joins her

Mary Can we go through it one more time ?
Gerry Of course.
Mary Where did you put the bag ?
Gerry Under the stairs.
Mary What do you put in it?
Gerry Two long flannel Catholic nighties. Nightgown. Slippers. New toothbrush, toothpaste, hairbrush, washbag. Make-up. Boxing gloves.
Mary Gerry!
Gerry Relax, Mary, the number of the taxi is on the wall beside the phone. There's a map of how to get here on the wall in the taxi company. Bernadette the controller, who's expecting in January herself by the way, has all the taxi drivers tormented working out the quickest route from here to Bedford Row. Bernadette, or whoever is on that day, will send a taxi to your mother's after we're on our way.
Mary And that's everything.
Gerry Yes.
Mary What about your sandwiches? It could be a long night.
Gerry I've got the feeling I won't really feel like eating, Mary. There is one avenue we haven't explored.

Mary Hmm?

Gerry Well, what if it happens on Tuesday ?

Mary I don't get you.

Gerry Well, what if it happens on Tuesday during the match?

Mary Oh, I get you.

Gerry Yeah, I mean, how will you contact me?

Mary No problem.

Gerry (*relieved*) Yeah?

Mary I'll lean over and say, "Gerry, we'd better go, the babies are coming".

Gerry Ah, Mary, you wouldn't be up to it, sur' Thomond Park'd be mad —
they've sold fourteen thousand tickets.

Mary gives Gerry a look

That's not quite what you meant, though, is it?

Mary shakes her head

'Cause I won't be at the game.

Mary nods her head

Look, Mary, I've it all worked out. Your mother'll come round; I'll only
be gone for two hours.

Mary Two hours. Are you tellin' me you'd let Lanky go off to the pub on
his own after the game? You would stumble in here at two in the mornin'.
You could miss the whole thing.

Gerry I won't, Mary, swear to God.

Mary Gerry, there are some things in life more important than rugby ...

Gerry Mary, no child of mine would have the bad manners to be born during
an important rugby match.

Mary The world doesn't turn revolve around Shannon Rugby Club, Gerry.
Has it got you a job?

There is a pause. Gerry is chastened

What are we going to do? Twins? Jesus, Gerry, twins!

Gerry We'll be grand, Mary. I am lookin', Mary, you know that. But there's
nothin'. Not a thing. (*Beat*) There might be somethin' in Krups in a few
months. We'll be looked after Mary. You know that.

Mary I don't want to be looked after, Gerry; I want a life. (*Beat*) Don't go
to the game Gerry. Please.

Gerry I won't. (*He breaks away*)

Mary Promise ?

Gerry It'll be fine, Mary, I promise.

Gerry becomes Dan Canniffe; Mary returns to the benches

Scene 11

Donal Canniffe is joined by his father Dan Canniffe. Donal Canniffe moves DR, *Dan* DL; *a spot comes up on each of them. They are on the phone*

Dan Hallo!

Canniffe Hallo, Dad.

Dan Ah, Donal, how are you keeping ?

Canniffe Ah, I'm in good form, Dad. I'm ringing from the hotel in Limerick.

Dan Oh yes, I understand you're to be Captain on the day.

Canniffe Ah, yeah, but sure the team runs itself anyway.

Dan They're a good team too, the All Blacks, very big I understand. You'll have your work cut out for you from the start.

Canniffe Well, yes, but it should be a great game. Actually, that's why I'm ringing: I've a few tickets left — I was wondering did you want them?

Dan Well, actually, I was talking to your brother about that, and I don't think I'll go. The ould angina's been at me a bit so I'd better take it easy.

Canniffe Are you feeling all right in yourself?

Dan Ah, yes, only every now and again, you know.

There is an awkward pause

So are you nervous?

Canniffe I suppose I ... I'm not too nervous about the game as such, but, you know, you don't want to let people down, like.

Dan Ah, once it starts you'll be grand. I remember in the '34 All Ireland. We were playing against Limerick and the great Mick Mackey. There was a lot of talk about Mick Mackey's magic hurley, because he was the first to run with the ball balanced on his stick; sure, now, every young fellow is doing it but back in '34 no-one had seen anything like it. Well, I'll tell you, once the game started it didn't matter a damn, you just got on with it and did your job same as anyone else.

Canniffe But ye didn't win the game though, Dad.

Dan No. As it turned out Mick Mackey did have a magic hurley!

They both laugh

Dan Well, win or lose, sur' we'll see you next weekend.

Canniffe OK.

Dan Good luck on Tuesday, Donal. Keep the head.

Canniffe Thanks, Dad, see you soon.

The spot on Canniffe goes out

Dan Good luck, son.

The spot on Dan fades slowly and then an interior setting, with an orange glow, comes up

SCENE 12

Tom Kiernan's last talk before the game

The Shannon players come forward and sit. They are watching a video

Kiernan These are the danger men. At right wing: Stu Wilson.

A spot comes up UC and the actor playing Wilson moves into the spot — "the TV spot" — and runs on the spot in slow-motion, as if he is in the middle of a game

Twenty-three. Six foot. Thirteen-and-a-half stone. Experienced. Sixteen games for New Zealand, five tests. Will run in tries from all over the pitch. This is a dangerous player for us. Incredible upper body strength can smash through tackles. The ball sticks to his hands. Brilliant acceleration; if he gets behind us at all he will be very hard to stop. Watch him here coming into the line from the blind side, at speed, between the out half and first centre — breaks the tackle and in for a try.

Wilson dives and scores a try DS

He has to be stopped, dead, first time, every time. BJ Robertson.

Wilson moves out of the TV spot and is replaced by Robertson

Best centre in the world.

Robertson acknowledges the compliment

Twenty-six. Six-one.

The actor playing Robertson realizes he's not 6'1" and goes on tippy toes

Thirteen stone. Seventy-two games for New Zealand. Thirty-three tests. This man has achieved everything worth achieving in rugby and he's still young. Tremendous instinct can turn a game in seconds. A brick wall in defence. Mercurial in attack.

Robertson moves out of the TV spot

Gary Knight.

The actress moves into the TV spot. The other actors laugh at her. She mimes ripping out someone's heart, eating it, then spitting it out during the following

Six foot two. Seventeen-and-a-half stone. Eight games, five tests. Bronze medal for Wrestling at the Commonwealth games. Doesn't really need elaboration, does it?

The actress returns to her place

That's the enemy. (*He turns off the video*) Here's how we beat them. (*He flicks on the lights in the room*) We surprise them. It's physics, lads. Use their own power against them. Turn the scrums. Bring down the rucks. Stop them building any momentum. There's been a lot of talk about fifteen-man rugby. Well, if their centres or flankers try any of that we will bury them. Good close pressure. Stop them playing. Let me tell you, lads, there is as much beauty and poetry in a well-timed well-executed tackle as there is in a three quarter break to the line with a try under the posts. A good tackle is truthful and honest. It is devoid of ego. A hard tackle is carried out for the team. Play till your hearts break, Tony; take whatever chances you can. But most important of all lads remember this: (*beat*) it's only a game.

They all laugh, then face the audience, growling. They freeze

SCENE 13

A strange version of the orange interior lighting comes up

The Gerry actor, smiling, becomes the Girl with the Harp; he plays an imaginary harp. The cast becomes the Bunratty Singers and sing a verse of "The Colleen Bawn"

All   Oh, Limerick is beautiful as everybody knows.
              The river Shannon full of fish beside that city flows.
              But it's not the river nor the fish that preys upon my mind

Nor with the town of Limerick,
Have I any fault to find.

The Lights cross-fade to a normal interior state DR

Two of the Bunratty "girls" become Haden and Wilson and move into the DR
area

Wilson Have you tried the mead?
Haden No. Russ said we weren't allowed.
Wilson Me neither. How's your chicken?
Haden Fine.
Wilson Those costumes are pretty sexy.
Haden Are you sure you haven't had any booze?
Wilson Some of these girls are very talented.

*Wilson waves at one of the "girls" who flirts with him much to his delight and
the chagrin of one of her colleagues*

Haden I wouldn't know.
Wilson Aw, come on, just 'cause you're married doesn't mean you can't
appreciate beauty when you encounter it.
Haden Try telling that to my wife!
Wilson Oh, yeah, the locals are pretty friendly, actually.
Haden Yeah.
Wilson Do you know what a high ding is?
Haden A high ding?
Wilson Yeah.
Haden No.
Wilson Well, that sexy one there told me we're going to be presented with
one during the game.
Haden We're going to get a high ding during the game ? That'll be nice.
That'll be nice. What's this bet you have going with BJ?
Wilson Oh, just that I'll run in twice as many tries as him on Tuesday.
Haden What if he doesn't score?
Wilson I don't get you.
Haden Well, if he doesn't score you can't win. (*Beat*) Twice nothing is
nothing. So to win the bet all he has to do is not score. Even if you score
twenty points Tuesday, technically if he scores zero he'll win the bet.
And if you both get zero you could say you've won your bet but he
could also say that you have the same score. It could get messy, mate.

A spot comes up on the Girl with the Harp

The Girl with the Harp (*improvizing a sad, pretentious tune and
     accompanying herself by plaintively strumming her instrument*)
          *Bhi bobilin mor aige
          Ach do fuar se bas
          Agus bhi se marbh ansin.* *
          (* Translation: He had a big penis
          But he died
          And then he was dead.*)

The Lights change to a daytime exterior setting

Haden returns to the benches

Scene 14

*Wilson becomes a dog, Sinbad. The Bunratty Singers become Irene, David,
Rodney and Marjorie, a group of posh Cork supporters gathered round a car,
eating sandwiches and having tea from flasks out of the boot*

Irene Well, Rodney, you did very well to get parking so near the ground; we
     should never have doubted you.
David Well, do you know I was beginning to doubt you myself? I've
     never seen so many people up for a game. Oh, Rodney, do you have the
     tickets?
Rodney Oh, yes, only terrace tickets I'm afraid, ladies. But it's as well to be
     in the thick of it at these games, soak up the local colour.

The ladies are unimpressed

     God, Marjorie, these sandwiches are marvellous. What have you in them?
David Oh, now, Rodney you're on dangerous ground there. Those sandwiches
     are top secret. If Marjorie told you the recipe I'd have to kill you myself.
Marjorie Thank you, Rodney — oh, nothing special, just ham and a bit of
     French cheese. David wanted to stop here in Limerick for something to eat.
     Well, I wouldn't hear of that at all. Pay out good money for a bit of leathery
     old meat and soggy lettuce? At least with my sandwiches you know where
     you stand. Will you try a sausage roll, Irene ?

Irene pats her tummy to indicate that she's had enough

David Keep an eye out for Peter and Audrey. Peter's got one of those new
     Saabs, so he should be easy to spot.

Rodney I'll tell you they're lovely cars, but you know were you stand with a Granada.

Spider comes DS to them

Watch your bags, girls, I don't like the look of this laddie.
Spider Give us a sangwhidge 'illya?
David Clear off now, let you.
Spider That's a lovely car you have, mister. What is it, a Cortina?

David almost chokes on his tea

Rodney No, sonny, that's a Granada.
Spider Are ye going to the match? Is that where ye're going?
David That's right. Now go on off about your business, you.
Spider I don't have a business, mister, I'm only twelve. Do you want me to look after your car for ye while ye're in at the game?
Rodney Well, you see, we thought about that so we brought our dog Sinbad with us to protect it. Isn't that right, Sinbad?
Marjorie God, Rodney, you think of everything!
Rodney Oh, yes, Sinbad will look after it for us. You'd be taking your life in your hands now if you were to cross him.

The dog advances menacingly on Spider. Spider tickles him playfully, much to Rodney's displeasure

Get in the car, Sinbad!

The dog gets into the car and sticks its nose out the window

Spider God, he's a lovely dog, mister. My brother has a alsatian.

The Cork people tidy up the car

David That's lovely for him. Cheerio, now.

The Cork people make to leave

Spider Hey, mister, can your dog put out fires, can he?

The Cork people freeze

Marjorie I think you'd better pay the lad, David.

The Lights change to a night-time exterior setting

They all return to the benches

SCENE 15

Gerry comes DS *alone, worried. A moment later, Lanky moves to him*

Lanky Gerry, we're sorted.
Gerry How?
Lanky I have tickets.
Gerry Where did you get 'em?
Lanky You know how I'm always complaining about my ma and da at breakfast?
Gerry What with the ——
Lanky Funeral notices, yeah. (*He mimics his father*) "I see Dermot O'Connor's after dying." (*He mimics his mother*) "Is that right?" (*Father*) "Oh, yes." (*Mother*) "Wasn't he married to one of the Collinses from Rosbrien?" (*Father*) "No, that's a different Dermot O'Connor; this fellah had a gammy leg, used to work as a clerk over in Matterson's, had a cousin killed as a merchant seaman during the emergency ..." (*Mother*) "Oh, yes, I haven't seen him in an age!" (*Father*) "Well, he's dead, now."
Gerry What's this got to do with the tickets?
Lanky Well, it gave me an idea.

The Lights change to a dark interior setting

The actor last seen as Spider becomes an old, male, relative of the deceased; Gerry becomes a priest

Lanky (*addressing an unseen mourner out front*) I'm very sorry for your trouble. (*He repeats this twice, then moves on to talk to the Relative*)

The Relative takes some snuff then offers some to Lanky. Lanky takes some then sneezes

Lanky (*with tears in his eyes*) Poor old Dermot O'Connor. He'll be sorely missed.
Relative Did you know him well?
Lanky Ah yeah, yeah. I used to meet him out walkin'.

Relative Really, I didn't think he was a great man for the walkin' what with
    the ...
Lanky The leg, yeah, yeah ... Well, I'd be out walkin', he'd be out sitting
    on the same bench every week over on Barrington's pier.
Relative That's right. Oh, he loved the bit of fresh air.

Beat

Lanky Great man for the rugby, of course.
Relative Oh, he was, oh yeah. Oh, a divil for Garryowen all the same.
    Yourself?
Lanky Oh, yeah, Garryowen all my life. Hurray for Garryowen, isn't that
    the way. 'Tis funny really, 'cause there was a few of us to be going together
    on Tuesday; he'd have loved the game, 'tis a shame really.
Relative Sur' ye can still go anyway, can't ye?
Lanky Ah, yeah. (*He sighs audibly, twice*)
Relative Well, can't ye?

Beat

Lanky Well, that's just the thing, you see. 'Twas Dermot bought the tickets
    for the three of us, and now he's ...(*He indicates the corpse*)
Relative Oh, I have you!

Beat

    Wait there a minute.
Lanky Ah, no.
Relative No, no.
Lanky No, no, no.
Relative No, no, no, no NO!
Lanky OK.

The Lights change to a night-time exterior setting

The Relative goes

    (*To Gerry*) Five minutes later he comes back with two tickets. I explained
    that we hadn't paid for them, so the widow gets one-sixty towards the cost
    of the wake and everyone is happy.
Gerry But how did you know he had tickets?
Lanky Well, remember out in Dooradoyle, the girl pointed to a fellah and
    said he's after takin' the last of the tickets?
Gerry Yeah.

Lanky Well he had a limp, and between ourselves he wasn't lookin' too
healthy, so I thought I'd chance my arm.

Gerry You're an awful man.

Lanky So we're sorted.

Gerry (*unconvincingly*)Yeah.

Lanky So what's the problem?

Gerry No problem! (*He pants, preparing for the Haka, and becomes an All
Black*)

SCENE 16

The Lights change to a spooky setting for the Haka

The rest of the cast joins Gerry and Lanky and they become the All Blacks

Mourie Kia mo.

The Lights change again to a different spooky setting

All Heeeeee.

Mourie Ringia packia.

The Lights come up full and white

All   Ka mate, ka mate, ka ora, ka ora,
                 Ka mate, ka mate, ka ora , ka ora.
                 Tenei te tangata puhuruhuru,
                 Nana i tiki mai whaka whiti te ra.
                 Up ane upane,
                 Up ane kaupane,
                 Whiti te ra. Heee!*

**For pronunciation, see p. viii*

The cast becomes the crowd, chanting

Gerry Come on, Munster.

The Lights change to a bright cold exterior setting with a spot DR

All Munster, Munster.

BBC Commentator (*stepping into the* DR *spot*) ... and Tony Ward kicks off
into the clear blue Munster sky.

The DR *spot is cut*

The ball is in the air ...
Wilson My ball. (*He leaps* DC *and grabs the ball*)

Dennison and Locky tackle Wilson. The whole cast falls DL, *then get up straight away and form a ruck*

On me! On me!

Moss Keane breaks through to the front of the ruck

Moss Keane I'm takin' the ball or your fingers you ugly sheepshaggin' bastard. (*He grabs Stu's hand*)

Wilson screams

Moss Keane becomes Mary and is held up by the others. She is giving birth and screaming. Some of the rugby players become nurses

Nurse Push, Mary!
Mary Ahhhh. Where's Gerry ?

Mary is dropped on her feet

All (*as Mary hits the floor*) Scrum!

Four actors form a scrum — two props, and behind them two second rows. Two scrum halves stand US *behind the second rows. McLoughlin (Locky) is the Munster front row prop, with the Gerry actor behind him and Canniffe as scrum half; Ashworth is the New Zealand prop, Wilson the second row and the actress, the scrum half*

The scrum is lit from floor level with a warm fill from above

McLoughlin It is I, Locky. Red of hair and jowl.

The scrum engages

The first scrum. All Blacks put in. One thousand seven hundred pounds of pressure, going through my shoulders. I try to get over Ashworth, screw his shoulders towards the earth; if he is beneath me, it breaks up their drive. Come on, you bastard, down you go.

The two props struggle, trying to bring each other to the ground

The ref. is lookin' for a high elbow. But I do it with a hand on the shoulder.
Make it look like the other guy is bringin' it down.

The scrum goes down

Canniffe Ref.! (*Under his breath*) For fuck's sake.
McLoughlin Many's the penalty try I've scored for Shannon with that little
trick!

They form another scrum. This time Ashworth faces the audience

Ashworth This guy is strong. He's already got over me once. He won't win
this battle. Scrum low and tight. Wriggle, break his purchase. The ball's in,
it's swept back. We hold. Make the bastards wait. The lock guards the ball
with his foot. Now we make them pay. Drive. Driiive …
All (*groaning*) Drive, Munster. Drive, break.

The scrum moves R *in two heaves*

Scene 17

*The scrum half (the actress) gathers the ball and makes a blindside break.
She is tackled and held aloft as Mary in the labour ward*

Mary Ahhhh!
Gerry (*moving from his scrum position to* DR) Jesus, Mary ——
Mary Gerry !
Gerry — and Joseph, Munster, they're driving you all over the fuckin' field.
Can't ye at least drive them back on their ball, ye shower of oul' women?

Ashworth becomes David of the posh Cork people. He joins Gerry

David You know, I think you might have a point there. If they can't drive
them off their own ball we could be in trouble.
Gerry We have to win it in the scrums though, don't we? We haven't the
height in the ——
All Line out.

The Lights change to a cold exterior setting

*It's a Munster throw-in. Haden and Ashworth for the All Blacks, Moss Keane
and the Gerry actor for Munster stand in two rows,* UR, *facing* US. *Pat Whelan
faces them as the Munster hooker. Canniffe stands off the mats* R, *level with
the first player in the lineout*

During the following, the cast without lines chants "Munster Munster"

Canniffe Soda cake, ball.

Pat Whelan (*unable to hear as the crowd is too loud*) Say again!

Canniffe Soda cake, ball.

Canniffe throws the ball in. Haden jumps; the other actors fall on one knee, arms held aloft

Haden Andy Haden's ball. Got it. Easy ball, boys.

Moss Keane and Canniffe bind on Haden. Ashworth peels off UL

Moss Keane (*to Haden*) Give me the ball or I'll break your face.

Ashworth Get off him, you savage.

Ashworth punches Moss Keane and everyone groans

The Lights brighten

Ashworth Break!

Ashworth becomes Donaldson and whips the ball out. Man by man the ball goes out the line

The players say their name as they pass the ball along

Donaldson Donaldson.

Canniffe becomes Robertson

Robertson Robertson.

Haden becomes Mourie

Mourie Mourie.

Moss Keane becomes McKechnie

McKechnie McKechnie.

Canniffe becomes Williams

Williams Williams.

Pat Whelan becomes Wilson

Wilson Wilson. (*He moves in an arc from* UL *to* DL *and runs in slow motion*)

Williams becomes Lanky and takes up a position in a spot DR

Robertson becomes Gerry and moves into a spot off the mats DL

Wilson moves up the pitch. The other actors form a line UC *just off the mats*

Gerry Oh, no, Wilson's comin' in off the blind side. He's clear through — oh, Jesus, the speed! Tackle him for fuck's sake. Who's there? It's Seamus Dennison — he'll never stop him.

Gerry becomes Seamus

The actors produce sounds of breathing and running

During the following, Seamus speaks more quietly when Kiernan, Lanky and Wilson are speaking

Seamus I'll tackle any man, anywhere on the pitch, he'll go down and I'll get up before him; first back in to play, no matter who I hit. (*He repeats this as a mantra until his next scripted line*)

Mourie becomes Tom Kiernan and moves down from UC *to talk into Seamus's ear*

Kiernan You're too small, Seamus — some of these lads have four stone on you. If they break through in the centre, they'll piss on us.
Lanky Dennison will never stop him. Wilson is six foot, he has two stone on Seamus Dennison.

The actress and the Ward actor perform the Haka US

Dennison My mind over his. If he knows when I'm going to hit him he has the advantage. Hit him a yard before he expects it. Use his momentum against him.
Kiernan He'll come into the line from the blindside at speed.

The Lights come up very brightly

If he's not put down first time he's through for a try. Breaks the tackle and through for a try. First time.

Wilson We're here to honour our country, we're here to honour our
  country ...
Seamus Ahhhhhhh.

*The tackle happens. The action is lit from behind. Seamus and Wilson crash
into each other c and lie still on the ground. A moment of stillness*

Lanky Jesus, he's killed him.

The Lights change to a cold exterior setting

Lanky becomes Canniffe and approaches Seamus

Canniffe (*under his breath*) Seamus, get up. Get up, for fuck's sake. You've
  shaken the whole ground — don't blow it now. Up first.
Mourie Get up, Stu. Your little sister is bigger than that guy!
Canniffe "I'll put any man down, anywhere on the pitch and get up first" —
  remember?

Canniffe offers Seamus a hand. Seamus waves it away and gets up

Canniffe Good man, ya boy, ya!
Mourie Wilson, get on your feet!

*Seamus and Canniffe walk back to their position. Seamus can barely walk.
Wilson gets up and staggers back into position. The players look at each other*

Canniffe (*to Seamus*) Are you all right ?

Seamus nods

Seamus NO. My shoulder's completely banjaxed.
Canniffe They don't know that though, do they? Jesus, Seamus you've
  really rattled them. (*He pats Seamus on the bad shoulder*)

Seamus nearly dies

Seamus Well, they won't try that again in a hurry.

A weird orange interior lighting state comes up

All apart from Wilson become the Bunratty Singers in Wilson's head

Singers (*singing*) Oh, Limerick is beautiful as everybody knows.
      The river Shannon full of fish …

On "fish " a singer becomes Mourie and slaps Wilson on the face

All return to being players

The Lights return to the cold exterior setting

Wilson shakes his head

Mourie You all right, bro? You need a drink?
Wilson There's something weird here, Graham. I think they're all mad. That
      little fellow is smiling at me. It's like he enjoyed it.
Canniffe Keep your heads, boys. Just put them down and take your chances.

During the following they all kneel in a line c, *facing the audience, their arms
in the air*

All Ball went forward. Scrum. Out half clears. Line out.

They react to the ball being thrown in from DC

Foley (*jumping up in slow motion*) Brendan Foley jumps highest and grabs
      the ball.
      On me, lads. On me.

The actors bind c *on Brendan Foley. Brendan Foley hands the ball to
Canniffe and moves out* L *to become Ward*

A spot comes up DR

Gerry (*moving into the spot*) Good man Brendan Foley, keep it tight, boy.

The spot is cut

Canniffe Canniffe passes.
Ward Ward takes. Good easy ball into my chest.

A spot comes up on Ward and Kiernan

The players freeze c

Kiernan (*coming out of the freeze; turning*) We're used to your little ways,
      Tony. Keep them guessing. If we can get them going backwards, all the
      better.

The spot is cut

Ward (*unfreezing*) What's the option? A grubber kick through the centres, a Garryowen to put our pack charging down on the full back? Or a pass out the line? Then it becomes clear — it is the most obvious thing in the world. Keep them guessing. A short lob over the heads of the halfbacks.

The players c break in slow motion. Wilson becomes Bowen and bursts through. The others chase him on the spot in slow motion

Bowen Jim Bowen rushes on to it.

A spot comes up on Gerry DR

Wardy, you beauty. (*He freezes c*)
Gerry What's that jumped-up little Dublin fucker after doing ? Wilson is rushing on to the ball. If he collects it he's through.

A spot comes up c

Bowen, c, looks at the flight of the ball. He runs in slow motion

Bowen The bounce of a rugby ball is unpredictable. It can break your heart. When the ball goes to ground between Bowen and Wilson the match is in the balance. Whoever collects will score. Earthworms and physics dictate the outcome. Today even the earthworms are shouting for Munster.
All as Worms Munster.
Bowen My ball. Run. Keep your head. Eyes open, look for the cover. Full back. Jink inside then outside. He's gone. Inside the twenty-two. I can see the line. The covers gaining ground. A hand on my shoulder. Hold them off. Turn inside. Make the ball available. A red blur. Christy Cantillon takes the pass. He's made eighty yards in eleven seconds. Jesus, he's through. He's through. We've scored.

The Lights return to the cold exterior setting

All Yesssssss.

They all come c, cheering, then hoist Mary in the air. The players, apart from Mary, become Nurses

Mary Aaahhhhhhhrrghhh. (*She breathes noisily through the following*)

The Lights change to a spot c on Mary and another on the Ward actor

Nurses Push, Mary!

*A Nurse becomes Ward and lines up to kick the conversion in front of Mary
and the Nurses*

Ward Thomond Park is a very special place during a penalty kick or a
conversion. No matter whose kick it is there will be absolute silence. (*He
hushes Mary*)

Mary quietens down considerably

If some eejit calls out he will be hushed by angry Limerick voices who feel
their honour and hospitality are at stake. Today the air is still.

Mary stops making any noise

This is an easy kick. Twenty yards out under the posts, a chance to put
another two points up against the greatest team in the world.
Mary Ahhhh.

The Nurses are anxious

Nurse Relax, Mary. I know it's hard. Don't push, the cord is around the
baby's neck. Just breathe. Breathe. Calm.
Mary What's wrong? What's the matter, what's happening?
Nurse 2 There's nothing wrong. Just don't push for a moment.
Mary Aarghhhhhhhhh.
Nurse (*urgently*) Don't push!

The Lights return to the cold exterior state

Ward kicks the ball

*Everyone cheers and moves C to become the crowd. Gerry is in the middle.
Ward becomes David, Mary becomes Marjorie; they stand to Gerry's left.
Lanky is to his right*

All Yessssssss!
Gerry Yesssss, yesssss, that Tony Ward is a fuckin' genius. Six-nil and only
twelve minutes gone. Come on, Munster.
David Do you know that's the first try scored against the All Blacks in this
tour? And we're the first northern hemisphere team to take the lead over
an All Black side since Wales in 1954 and even they didn't do it till the

second half. Of course that was actually a penalty try; to see a try like that from play you'd probably have to go back to 1933, against Scotland for God's sake.

Marjorie Oh, David, you're an awful man for the statistics. Here, ask your friend would he like a little drop of that?

David Care for a snifter, lad?

Gerry God, yeah.

David hands Gerry a hip flask. Gerry drinks; it nearly burns the throat off him

Beat

That's great stuff, what is it?

David Brandy and port. Hits the spot.

Gerry Thanks very much. (*He indicates he'd like to give some to Lanky*)

Gerry gives Lanky the flask; Lanky drinks and produces an exact replica of what happened to Gerry

Jesus, a fellah could get used to this.

Lanky Yeah.

Gerry What's wrong witcha?

Lanky They're only leading us up the garden path, though, isn't that all?

Gerry What?

Lanky Six-nil against the All Blacks: like, who are they kiddin'? We're goin' to get a landin' now. I think scoring against them, it'll only annoy them. I'm telling you I wouldn't like to be facing into this kick-off.

Gerry Would you ever relax. You spent too long at that feckin' wake. Here give us that. (*The flask*) Come onnnn Munnsterrrrr!!

Gerry hands the flask back to David

David (*trying to imitate Gerry*) Come on, Munster!

SCENE 18

David becomes Ashworth

Ashworth All Black ball.

Floodlights come up

Ashworth catches the ball. All the other actors run backwards US. *Ashworth is confused, waiting for something to happen. Then the Munster players*

charge down on him, stamping on him as they go over him. Ashworth
screams. When they have passed him, three actors turn US *and two face* DS,
their heads appearing between the legs of the actors facing US

Ashworth now becomes Wayne Graham and hides behind the group US

Seamus Munster ball, lads. We have.
Canniffe We have, lads. Drive.
All Drive.
Canniffe (*secretly to the lock — the actress*) Hold it in.
Donaldson (*played this time by the Wilson actor*) Got to be disciplined.
   Canniffe will try to lure me offside with a dummy.

Canniffe slaps the actress on the arse and feigns a pass

Canniffe Break !!

Graham pops up from behind the group and growls

Donaldson Come on, All Blacks, they're holding us back. Let's get stuck
   into them.
Canniffe We have, we have. Munster ball.

Graham beats his chest like Tarzan and dives into the ruck

Donaldson An All Black hand is on the ball.
Canniffe Get him out of there.

Moss Keane stamps on the hand. Graham tears the Munster players out of
his way as he speaks

Graham Wayne Graham, six-two, fifteen stone. Takes a little turn! (*He*
   takes a little turn and tries to punch Canniffe)

A whistle blows

Canniffe Yes!

All the actors become the All Blacks and walk backwards

Mourie (*furiously*) How many times have you been told that they won't wear
   that here, Wayne?
Graham (*showing Mourie his sore hand*) Yeah.

They all line out at the back of the mats facing DS

Mourie Yeah. Now, wake up; we could be in trouble here if we don't get the finger out. Now we are going to take the game to them. If they hit hard, hit them harder. Someone run at that little fucker Dennison and teach him a lesson. Right, now, let's charge down this penalty.Ward's sliced it.

McKechnie leaps forward. The rest of the players freeze

McKechnie McKechnie's balllllllll. Tracking the ball as it comes. Thinking ahead. Mourie to my left. Robertson directly behind me. The cover is coming fast; if I call for a mark it slows down the game in our twenty-two, giving them the advantage—no, the thing to do is launch it right back down their throats. Kick into the stratosphere so that whatever poor deluded Munster bastard ends up underneath it, also ends up underneath the flesh and studs of our All Black pack. The wings are closing but I've got time. I'm an All Black; all-conquering, ravaging warrior. Munster will rue the day they scored against us. (*She catches the ball then, agonizingly, knocks it on*)

The others hold their heads in despair

Oops.
Mourie Oh, God, McKechnie, you fool. A knock on under the posts. Against a team with Tony Ward? (*He turns to the team*) Come on, lads, let's drive them up the park. Eye contact with McKechnie, the loneliest man in the world. Try to be positive. Cover the truth. All Blacks don't make mistakes. Don't drop balls. Don't give the opposition any soft chances. This is total rugby. Open rugby. A beautiful game played in a hard, uncompromising, exhilarating way. Clap McKechnie on the shoulder, he's dying inside. Try not to do that again, eh?

A spot comes up DR

Seamus becomes Gerry and moves into the DR *spot*

Gerry Go way ourra that; you wouldn't catch your mother.

The lighting changes: the stage is lit from below; the orange colour comes up

All Scrum down.

SCENE 19

We see the scrum head on. Three players form the front row — from R to L,
McLoughlin, Knight and Robertson — and we see the faces of the second row
— Canniffe and Tucker — as their heads come between the thighs of the front
row. The scrum half (the Ward actor with a New Zealand accent) stands to
one side

McLoughlin Feet dig in, claw at earth.
Robertson Shoulder on buttock.
Canniffe Cheek on thigh.
Tucker Arms under.
Knight Arms over.
Seamus Steam rising.
Ward Breath foaming.
McLoughlin Shoulders twisting, voices cursing.
Knight Hooker watching.
Seamus Props crushing.
Tucker Necks aching.
Ward Deep Heat burning.
Canniffe Vaseline cooling.
McLoughlin Tempers fraying.
Seamus Fists flying.
Ward Scrum halfs waiting.
Canniffe Flankers farting.
Knight Throats burning,eyes streaming.
McLoughlin Scrum turning.
Ward Ref. whistling.
Seamus Props rising.
Tucker Ref. talking.
Ward (*in a Welsh accent*) No more biting, gouging, punching, or swearing,
   you.
Robertson Right, Ref., down we go.
McLoughlin Feet dig in. Claw at earth.
Canniffe Shoulder on buttock.
Tucker Cheek on thigh.
Knight Props crushing, hooker watching, arm tapping, hooker sweeping.
Canniffe Scrum half spinning.
Ward (*now as himself*) Ward taking, looking. Drop goal on.

The Lights return to the cold exterior setting

Robertson breaks from the scrum and moves DC. The other actors run
backwards in slow motion

Robertson Running, arms outstretched, anticipate flight path of ball.
Ward Head up, head down, drop, and strike spinningly.
Robertson Arcingly, achingly between the posts.
Ward Whistle.
Robertson Three points.

All freeze apart from Ward

Ward Yesss. Inside, pleasure explodes in my brain. Wohooooooooo!
Outside, turn and grimace. Rugby demands modest, humble celebrations
of joy. Extravagant celebrations by scoring players are considered from the
spirit of rugby. Emotion is best turned inward. To stoke the fire in the belly.
One or two players punch me in the small of the back or on top of the head.

The others do so, the blows getting more ridiculous and harder as they go on

It is manly acknowledgement of my skill. It hurts like hell but they mean
well.

Seamus kicks Ward in the backside

Seamus Good man, Wardy.

SCENE 20

They all go into a huddle C facing DS

All All Black pack.

*The lighting changes: the stage is lit from below; the orange colour comes
up*

*All but Mourie crouch and whisper the Haka quietly during the following
speech*

Mourie Right, boys, half-time approaches. We have to get points on the
board before the break. We will play the remaining time in their twenty-
two. Charge downfield after the kick-off. Keep it tight. Play nine man
rugby. Get the ball back in front of the mauls. Little jiggy runs by the
flankers. Keep it going forward.
Moss Keane Moss Keane's ball!

The Lights return to the cold exterior setting

The All Blacks engulf Moss Keane. He throws them off. They fall all over the stage. Mourie gets up DL *and grabs the ball*

Mourie   It's there for Graham Mourie.

The Lights change to a bright white setting

> He takes.
> Pack gathers.

The others bind on him. Moss Keane becomes Gary Knight and the others move from Mourie to bind on him

> Stay on my feet.
> Knight peels away.
> Release the ball.
> **Knight**   Knight
> Takes,
> Bursts past the cover.

Knight breaks free and the others fall back

> Turn as I fall.
> All Black ball.

Ashworth crouches C *facing* DS

Ashworth   Ashworth.

Wilson binds with Ashworth, masking him

Wilson   Wilson.

Knight lies back on Ashworth's back; he then hoists her on to him (so that, when he stands up later, she will remain on his back and vanish from view)

Gerry moves to the spot DR

Knight   Knight.

Johnstone binds left of Ashworth facing US

Johnstone   Johnstone gathers.
> Five metres out.
> Driive!

          One metre out!
          Driiiive!
All Puuussshhhh!

The Lights change to a spot C

Knight becomes Mary

Wilson switches position to be R *of Ashworth facing* L, *revealing Mary screaming on Ashworth's back. Wilson becomes Nurse 1, Johnstone becomes Nurse 2*

During the following, when we are in the game Ashworth straightens up, masking Mary; when we are in the labour ward he crouches down revealing Mary on his back

Mary appears over the maul

Mary Aaggghhhhhhh.
Nurse 1 Good girl, Mary, nearly there. Breathe.
Mourie Come on, driiive.
          Get your fucking hand off the ball.

Mourie punches someone in front of him. Mary reacts as though she has been punched

Mary Oh Jesus. Agggghhhhh.
Nurse 1 Come on, Mary, just a little more.
Mourie Mourie gathers.
          Two feet from the line.
          We're through.
Mary Agggghhhhhhhh.
Nurse 1 Push, Mary.
Gerry Jesus, Munster get it out of there.
Mary Jesus, Nurse get it out of there.
Mourie Driiiiiiive.
          We have.
          We have.
Nurse 1 Breathe, Mary.
          That's it.
          Now push!
Mourie Look up.
          I see an opening.

Ashworth turns to face us so Mary is facing the audience. Mourie runs behind them

Gerry Get rid of it, Munster.
Nurse 1   It's coming, Mary.
                 I can see the head.

Mourie's head appears between Ashworth's legs just under Mary; it looks as if she is giving birth to Mourie

Mourie I can see the line!
Nurse 2 One more push, Mary.
Mourie I have the ball. All I have to do is put it down.

Nurse 1 grabs Mourie's head

Nurse 1 I have the head; all you have to do is push it down.
Mourie Driiiive.
Mary Aaggghhhh.
Mourie We're through !

Mourie becomes the baby

Nurse Well done, Mary.

Nurse 1 slaps the baby and he cries

Nurse 1 becomes Greg Barrett. The baby's head is the ball. The other actors are confused

Barrett   Greg Barrett gathers for Munster.
                 Barrett kicks the ball away.

Barrett becomes Nurse 1 again, cradling the baby. The baby cries again

Nurse 1 You have a son, Mary. One down, one to go.
Mary Where's Gerry ?
All (*to the audience*) Half-time.

Black-out

Music: Staying Alive

ACT II
SCENE 1

The stage is in darkness

The actors take up their positions as at the end of Act I

Drums. We hear the baby scream and the drums cut out

The Lights come up; an interior state C

All (*as before*) Half-time.

The Lights change to a cold exterior setting

They all cheer and get into position as the crowd — Gerry, Lanky and David among them

Gerry Nine-nil. I wouldn't have missed this for anything. Not for a thing.
Lanky We're in trouble now, I'm tellin' you. This is not going to be pretty.
Gerry What the blazes are you on about? It's half-time. We're winning nine-nil.
Lanky That's my point. Look at the All Blacks. They're not happy, Gerry, not happy at all. They'll give our boys a hidin' now, no mistake about it.
David Can you not just enjoy the game?
Lanky No! I can't just enjoy the game. How many times have you watched Ireland play a great game? Get ahead. Run in a few tries. Only to be beaten by a jammy penalty in the last fifteen minutes. It's like those history stories Swifty used to teach us at the Model.
Spider Actor Oh, Jesus, they used to kill me.

During the following, the others react appropriately to Lanky's story

Lanky Exactly. The battle of fuckin' Kinsale. The English are trapped. The Spanish have the whole thing sewn up, Ireland is destined for a glorious victory. Freedom is in our grasp. But you know it isn't. Because you know we never really won. So you're waiting, hoping that they can win just this once. And old Swifty is loving it, he has us all built up. The armies are fit, the English are starving. This is it, one last glorious battle and Ireland is free!

The others cheer wildly; Lanky cuts them off

And then Swifty goes all pale. You think someone's done something. That the class is in trouble. Fuck it, he's nearly crying. Oh, there's a traitor in the Irish camp. And then you feel it in your little ten-year-old belly. The shrinking of hope. All is lost. The Irish armies are routed. The Irish do what they do best: glorious defeat. The joy and hope of the story, the glory of the plans just makes it worse. I'm tellin' you this is the same, Gerry. Munster are not going to beat the All Blacks. The greatest rugby team in the world? It's not going to happen Gerry, no fuckin' way.

Lanky becomes Donal Canniffe and, in the background, exhorts the Munster team

David becomes Tony Ward. A spot comes up, tight on his face

Ward This is bizarre. There are fourteen thousand people in the ground and every one of them is silent. The only sound I hear is Donal's voice …

The spot is cut

Canniffe Immortality, immortality; how much do we want it? We are forty minutes from history, lads.

A spot comes up on Tony Ward

Ward Oh, there's a baby crying in the stand and a dog barking in the distance. I catch the eye of people I know in the crowd. Friends of mine. They smile awkwardly and look away. Fourteen thousand people are holding their breath. They're afraid. They're amazed. They feel part of this. Because something is happening.

A spot comes up DR. *Canniffe moves into it. The Lights dim in the* DL *quarter of the stage*

Gerry becomes Dan Canniffe; Tony Ward becomes another old man (Friend 1) and the actor last seen as Graham Mourie becomes a third (Friend 2). They move to the DL *quarter of the mats and wait in darkness*

Canniffe becomes the BBC

BBC Commentator The crowd here are hushed, expectant. The referee has blown his whistle indicating to the teams that they are to line out in preparation for the second half. If the score-line were to stay as it is, well, that would be a very significant day for Irish rugby. Dan Canniffe, Donal's father, is listening to the match with his friends in Cork City.

SCENE 2

The light comes up DL *to reveal the three old men — with grumpy faces — standing at a bar drinking pints. Dan Canniffe is in the middle. They have been listening to the radio*

Friend 1 God, Dan, your young fellah must be fierce sore all the same. Them All Black fellahs are giving them a fierce going over.

Dan Ah. Donal is a big lad now, in fairness. He's well able to look after himself.

Friend 2 It'd be a shame for them to lose it now, after going so far ahead.

Dan Sur', who says they're going to lose anything?

Friend 2 Ah, that's not what I'm saying; I'm only saying that it's only half-time and it would be a cruel blow if it was snatched away from them. I mean sur', nine points is nothing. If the All Blacks convert an early try they're back in the game.

Dan Oh, you're right there, all right. I'd say the All Blacks will be swarming all over them early in the half. But if Munster can hold on even for ten minutes, I'd say they have it won.

Wilson charges into the pub

Wilson My ball.

The old men look at him quizzically

Friend 2 Who's your man?

The old men become players — Friend 1, Ashworth; Friend 2, Graham Mourie — and tackle Wilson; they all fall into a pile UR *with the remaining two players*

The Lights change to the cold exterior state

Mourie I can see the ball.
I can see an ear.
Bite it.
(*He bites the ear of a player in the ruck*)
Crunch it.
Another bite.
Chew it.
(*He takes a bigger bite*)

The whole pile screams and breaks up

> Ball out.

Mourie passes the ball to Ashworth

Ashworth Ashworth.
>   Head down.
>   Hand up.
>   Palm on face.

A player approaches Ashworth; he palms the player off

>   Shoulder on
>   Stomach.

A player approaches, collides with him and is thrown off

>   Munster hands on ball.

Another player grabs Ashworth from behind. During the following he snaps his head back and the player behind him screams, then throws him violently to the floor

>   Head back.
>   Bone on bone.
>   Crunch.
>   Tackled.

All the players form a ruck

Mourie   Ball, ball, ball,
>   Munster shirt covering ball.
>   Turn to ref.:
>   Play on?
>   Boot.
>   Studs.
>   Rake.

Mourie rakes his studs over the back of the offending player, Moss Keane. The ruck screams

>   Get out of there.
>   Dive in.

The Lights change to a warm setting UR

Mourie dives into the ruck UR; *it collapses on him. His head then pops out from under the mêlée*

Warm, dark, quiet in here. A world of bodies. Looks like chaos from outside. But in here every body has a function, every mind an objective. Attack. Protect. Ball. Break.

A cold exterior light comes up UL

Scene 3

The players dash frantically to the opposite side of the stage, then freeze

Tucker Tucker sees Mourie rake Moss Keane. He sees him gather the ball. Mourie is getting ready for another break. Time to break the momentum.

Tucker reaches for Mourie's groin. During the following, Tucker's hand and Mourie's groin are masked by one of the other actors

Seamus There is a moment of absolute clarity between the two men.
Mourie They share a secret.
Tucker Colm Tucker ——
Mourie — has Graham Mourie ——
Tucker — by the ——
Mourie — balls.

Mourie and Tucker perform a little ballet. Tucker keeps eye contact with Mourie, warning him to drop the ball. Every move Mourie makes is accompanied by extra pressure and knowing stares from Tucker. Eventually Mourie bows to the inevitable. The pressure becomes so extreme that he loosens his grip on the ball. Tucker sees this and pounces

Tucker Break!

The Lights cross-fade to a warm interior light DR

Scene 4

We are back with Dan Canniffe and his friends in Cork. The transition is immediate. Ward becomes Friend 1, Seamus becomes Dan Canniffe, Graham Mourie becomes Friend 2, shaking his leg as he makes the transition. They move DL

The others return to the benches

Friend 2 God Almighty, that's some pressure. The All Blacks are desperate for an early score.
Dan Pity about them.
Friend 2 They're very fond of putting the boot in, the All Blacks.
Friend 1 Well, of course, it's a different game altogether Down Under. Hard ground. Faster, I'd say. Them All Blacks'd stamp on you soon as look at you.
Dan Ah, our boys are well able for them. Sur' you wouldn't feel it during the game anyway. I broke my wrist once against Kildare and didn't feel it until the next morning.
Friend 2 You'd think they'd have the game on the telly all the same, wouldn't you?
Friend 1 Ah, sur' them RTE fellahs couldn't find their way to Limerick. Oh, no. If it's not happening in Dublin, it's not happening at all.
Dan I'll tell you, if Munster win this, there'll be some row.

A spot comes up DR. *The Lanky actor moves into it and becomes the BBC commentator. The old men freeze in position as if listening to the radio*

BBC Commentator The All Blacks pour through again. McGregor takes, drives up to the twenty-two. Willams is there; Williams has, Bill Osborne the substitute now. Munster are holding but the ball is there for the All Blacks. Mourie has it now. On the line, only Tucker to beat. He must score. He hesitates, looks for a man. Tucker has it. Tucker clears from his own line. Munster breathe again.

The Lights return to the cold exterior setting

BBC becomes Lanky, Friend 1 becomes David and joins Lanky. They are joined by Gerry, and an All Black Fan, played by the Stu Wilson actor, comes forward too

Gerry Fuck it, my heart can't take this, lads. Have you any of that brandy left, have you?
David (*drinking*) There's just a drop. That Graham Mourie fellow looks a bit pale, don't you think? (*He grabs his groin*)

The others all laugh

Gerry Well, it's very disappointing when you don't get points after pressure. If I was Graham Mourie I'd be shittin' myself. They take rugby very seriously in New Zealand, you know. They're very like the Japanese that way.

The others look at Gerry quizzically

I'd say if they lose here he'll have to kill himself.

Lanky (*shouting to the back of the stalls*) Where's your Haka now, you big ugly All Black bastard?

Gerry Come on, Munster. Jesus, Lanky he's coming over.

The others back off but Lanky fancies his chances. He comes right down to the front of the stage inviting the player to have a go

Lanky What are you lookin' at ? I'm not afraid of you.

The player obviously reacts

(*Backing off, terrified*) Gerry, Gerry.

All Black Fan That's John Black you're talkin' to there, matey. He works in an abattoir — he actually kills things for a living.

Lanky Have you been there all along? God ye're very quiet altogether. Good game, isn't it?

All Black Fan Ah, you lads enjoy it while you can. The All Blacks aren't going to be beaten by this shower.

Gerry So this is all just an act to get our little Munster hearts a-flutter?

All Black Fan Just a training run before we annihilate the national team.

Gerry So why haven't they scored?

All Black Fan They'll score.

Gerry But why haven't they scored yet ?

All Black Fan They'll score.

Gerry Have they ever been beaten nine-nil before?

All Black Fan The All Blacks don't get nil.

Lanky Tell me. Is there really more sheep than people in New Zealand?

All Black Fan Why?

Lanky Must be handy all the same.

They all laugh

SCENE 5

Lanky makes his way DR. A spot comes up on him. He becomes the BBC Commentator

Crowd (*mouthing*) Munster, Munster.

BBC Commentator All Black ball. The All Blacks have dominated the game from the sideline. They have won practically all their own ball. They have been camped in Munster's twenty-two for the last twenty minutes. Can they do something here? The backs are lined deep. The roar from the crowd is deafening. The chant — well, you can probably hear it — Munster, Munster.

The Lights come up on the crowd; cold

BBC holds his microphone out of the window

Crowd (*audibly*) Munster, Munster, Munster.

The BBC Commentator retracts the microphone; the Lights go down on the crowd

BBC Commentator John Black is having trouble hearing the call. Clouds of steam rise off the backs of the players, steel in their eyes. This has become an epic battle of wills. I have never seen a cauldron like it. This game is the essence of sport. Black throws.

The crowd react to the following as it is described

Munster haven't contested the ball! All Blacks gather. But Munster have gone for an eight-man drive. The All Blacks can't get the ball away, they're going backwards, across the line, up against the barrier wall. The crowd love it.

The Lights return to the cold exterior setting

Gerry   Come on, Munster. Drive them up the fuckin' field.
All   Munster, Munster.
               Munster, Munster.

Sinbad barks

Warm exterior lighting comes up DR

The crowd are confused. All but Spider and Sinbad leave the mats; they move DR

Scene 6

Spider talks to the dog

Spider Sinbad, I've got to go now. I'm on a mission. It's bonfire night and I know where we can get some old tyres. It's a place where people bring their tyres to be re-treaded, only some of them are so thrun down that they have to be thrun out. It's bonfire heaven, tyres and pallets and boxes, and there'll be no one around 'cause of the match. But I'll be back in half an hour to collect me money. Here's some bread. Feel free to do your business in there, they won't mind.

Sinbad barks

Spider Lovely dog !

Bright white exterior lighting comes up across the whole stage

SCENE 7

Sinbad becomes Stu Wilson

Wilson Wilson. (*He gets to his feet and moves* C. *He passes the ball to Spider*)

Spider becomes Mourie

Mourie Mourie.

Dunn comes forward

Mourie passes to Dunn and moves to the back of the stage

Dunn Dunn.
Ward There's an overlap.

Knight comes forward. Dunn passes to Knight

Knight Knight.

Dennison comes forward

Dennison Dennison tackles.

Dennison tackles Knight, knocking Knight US

Tony Ward comes forward and picks up the ball

Ward Munster ball. (*He kicks the ball*) Ward clears.

Warm exterior lighting comes up

Dennison becomes Gerry and all the others become the crowd, including David and Marjorie

Gerry (*chanting*) There is an isle
Crowd   There is an isle
Gerry   A bonny isle
Crowd   A bonny isle
Gerry   Stands proudly from
Crowd   Stands proudly from the sea.

Clap, clap, clap, clap

Gerry   And dearer far, than all this world.
              Is that dear Isle
Crowd   Is that dear Isle to me.
              Come on Munster!!!

Marjorie finds all of this very loud

Marjorie That little fellow is very keen on tackling, isn't he? Does that hurt? Who is he?
David That's Seamus Dennisson.
Marjorie And the big fellow with the red head?
David That's Gerry McLoughlin.
Marjorie And who does he play for?
David Shannon.
Marjorie Is that the nice rugby club we were in with Peter and Audrey ?
David (*whispering*) No, that was Garryowen.

At the mention of the odious word the other supporters react badly, staring at them

These gentlemen are Shannon supporters. They don't like Garryowen.
Marjorie How much longer is left, David? David! I mean, shouldn't we be thinking of going? The traffic will be only fierce. If we snuck out now we'd be away before the rush.

David looks at Gerry. Gerry sympathizes with him

David We might as well wait; it shouldn't be much longer now.
All Ruck.

Bright white lighting comes up

    Munster have.
Canniffe Canniffe spins
Ward   Ward takes.
           Garryowen.

The lighting turns orange

           The glory of sport.
           No-one knows what will happen next.

*All apart from Wilson become the "Munster meat" bearing down on Wilson
in extreme slow motion. The effect is comical*

Wilson   Under the ball.
           Keep your eye on it.
           Munster meat bearing down.

The other actors freeze

           Ball to ground.
           Awkward bounce.
           Right.
           Left.
           Twenty-two.
           Try line.
           Catch.
           Drop.
           Knock back.
           Munster meat.

The other actors growl at the audience

           Ground the ball.
           Five metre scrum.
           Oh no no.

Warm exterior lighting comes up

Scene 8

Wilson goes down on all fours; Spider, Jasper, Ferret and Dandy crawl under him and enter the tyre area

During the following, the other boys mime, following Spider's instructions

Spider   Tyres as far as ten year-old eyes can see!
               Pallets. Boxes. Oily rags.
               Work to be done.
               Team assembled.
               Jasper stands guard. Ferret and Dandy on either side of the fences.
               Pallets piled.
               Tyres rolled.
               Boxes thrown.
               Eyes, ears open for sign of big black dog ...
               or angry owner.
               Don't be greedy.
               Take what we can carry.
               Home by the alleys and lanes.
               Avoid the Guards and our mas and das.
               Pile it high,
               Rags and tyres on the bottom,
               Then wood and boxes,
               Then chipboard and damp carpet,
               Aerosols and Hilti bolts hidden nearby,
               Shrubs and bushes reaching for the sky;
               The architecture of arson.
               A big bad bastard of a bonfire.
Jasper The O'Mahonys will shit themselves!

The lighting brightens

The four boys form a tight group facing DS. *Jasper becomes Tony Ward; the other boys become players*

Canniffe Ball-out.
Ward Film star ball! Drop goal on.

The other actors lift the actress over their heads. She becomes the ball

All (*except Ball; shouting*) Bury him.

The Lights change to a general warm interior setting

Ball The ball soars, spinning end over end. Beneath me the open-mouthed stares of fans and players. Ahead of me, the spires of Limerick, a thousand chimneys release a thousand plumes of smoke into the blue Munster air. A crescendo of expectation and disbelief soars towards me. To my left the upright whooshes by, behind me a whistle. All around me a roar.

The Lights cross-fade to UR *and* DR *spots*

All Yeessssssss.

SCENE 9

The Stu Wilson and Canniffe actors lower the Ball to the floor; she becomes Mary and they become Nurses at her bedside, UR

Gerry moves into the spot DR

Nurse 1 Two boys Mary, seven and six pounds.
Nurse 2 Have you thought of names?
Mary Where's Gerry?

The Lights go down on Mary and the Nurses

Gerry   The names.
             Gerry McLoughlin,
             Les White,
             Moss Keane,
             Donal Spring,
             Colm Tucker,
             Pat Whelan,
             Brendan Foley,
             Tony Ward,
             Christy Cantillon,
             Moss Finn,
             Seamus Dennisson,
             Donal Canniffe,
             Greg Barrett,
             Jim Bowen,
             Larry Moloney.

All   Line out.

All the players drag themselves across the stage and line up for a line-out, facing the audience. Their breath is heavy. They stare wearily at the invisible thrower

Mourie Twelve-nil down, three minutes to go, and we're in our own twenty-two. Legs heavy. Four points for a try. Two for a conversion. Three for a penalty. Three for a drop goal.
         Come on, lads, we can still win this.
         There's only a couple of scores in it.
All   Ka mate, ka mate, ka ora, ka ora,
         Ka mate, ka mate, ka ora , ka ora.

They all jump for the ball

The Lights change to a cold exterior state. During the following the pace is as fast as it can be. The action moves all over the stage. Bodies are flung everywhere, recreating the last desperate moments of the game

Mourie Mourie takes, breaks forward, crashes into Donal.
All Spring.

The Lights come up very brightly

They all simulate a sharp shoulder block facing the audience

All Munster, Munster.
Knight Gary Knight takes, breaks forward.

Knight reacts as if tackled as the word is spoken

All Tackle. (*Beat*) Munster, Munster.
Wilson Now, it's Wilson; jinks, parries back to the pack.
All Munster, Munster. (*Beat*) Tackle.

Wilson reacts as if tackled. During the following lines each player takes the ball and is hit immediately, hitting the deck as the other actors shout "Tackle". They rise again immediately after being tackled

Graham Mourie becomes Andy Haden

Haden Haden gathers. Black shirts all around. Red mist in my eyes.

All Tackle.

Haden falls and gets up

McKechnie The ball is free. McKechnie.
All Tackle.

McKechnie falls and gets up

Robertson Robertson.
All Tackle.

Robertson falls and gets up

Graham Graham.
All Tackle.

Graham falls and gets up

Pack gather.

The Lights diminish to an area DC

Protect the ball carrier. Twenty-five metres out. Tackle !

Now the players form one big maul facing the audience with Andy Haden in the centre. When he is speaking the maul moves DS. When the cast shout "Munster" it goes backwards

Haden Whole pack behind me. Red mist in my eyes.
All Munster, Munster.
Haden But I can see it. We're nearly there.
All Munster, Munster.
Haden Ten yards out. Thighs screeching agony.
All Munster, Munster.
Haden Shoulders burning.
All Munster, Munster.
Haden Eyes streaming.

The maul is lit from floor level

Yes. Arms flailing. Yes, yes.
All Munster. Munster.

Haden stretches full length in an effort to reach the line

Haden Yes. We're there. Andy Haden is going to score.

They all freeze

  Oh no!

There is a long whistle. It's the worst sound Andy has ever heard. Andy falls to his knees, shattered

Haden We've lost.

The All Blacks take it in. They walk back disbelievingly to become the crowd

There is another long whistle

Lanky Gerry, we've beaten the All Blacks !

The Lights change to a cold exterior setting

All Yeeehhhh.
David Lanky, I love you.

David goes to plant a smacker on Lanky's lips which Lanky avoids

The others clap

Lanky becomes Donal Canniffe; he and Tony Ward shake hands with the defeated players

Canniffe Well played, good game. Well played.

The All Blacks are dignified in defeat

Wilson You didn't let us play, Tony.
Ward Thanks.
Wilson I didn't mean it as a compliment.

Wilson stomps off

Tony Ward is baffled at Wilson's lack of grace. Andy Haden becomes Graham Mourie and approaches Tony

Mourie Well done, Tony. It doesn't get much better than this. Stu will apologize for that later. He just takes takes it a bit personally. (*To Donal Canniffe*) Captain Fantastic.

Donal Canniffe becomes Lanky; he and Gerry and thousands of others invade the pitch

Gerry Well done, lads. Good man, Tony Ward.
All Tony!
Gerry Didn't the Shannon lads do us proud ?

The players try to fight their way through the crowd. The crowd faces another direction

Good man, Colm Tucker, Shannon can hold our heads high today!

Lanky becomes Donal Canniffe and gets away from the mêlée. Tony Ward becomes David

David Donal Canniffe!
All Donal!
David Come here to me, boy. A bit of Cork grit goes a long way. I'd say you'll remember this day for ever.
Canniffe Oh that's for sure.

Graham Mourie becomes a Spectator

Spectator How's poor Stu Wilson? Jesus, Seamus Dennisson nearly had you kilt. That'll teach you for tryin' to ride the Bunratty singers.
Crowd Hurray, Munster, Munster, Munster.
Spectator Mungo Gerry, what are you doin' here ?
Gerry Ah, same as yourself.

Gerry and the Spectator are swept apart. Gerry can no longer hear him

Spectator No, I'm serious. Your wife's at the hospital.
Gerry (*not hearing him but pretending he has*) Yeah, great. There'll be a few pints tonight.
Spectator She's havin' the twins like.
Gerry Yeah, it's mad.
Spectator Jesus, Gerry, your wife's at the hospital; she's havin' the babies!

Gerry (*still unable to hear him*) What?

Gary Knight has had enough of this. He lifts Gerry up by the lapels. The Spectator is swept away by the crowd

Knight Your wife is at the hospital having your children.
Gerry How did you know that?
Knight Go!

Knight throws Gerry away from him

Crowd   Munster, Munster, Munster.
              Munster, Munster, Munster.

Gerry appears between the legs of the crowd

Gerry Get out of my way. Can't you see I'm in a hurry? For fuck's sake ——

The crowd freezes

— it's only a game.

The crowd carries on as before

Lanky appears

Lanky Gerry, what are you doin' here? Mary's havin' the twins.
Gerry I know.
Lanky Well, maybe you should think about goin', like.
Gerry What are you cryin' about?
Lanky Somethin' in my eye! It's great though.

Gerry and Lanky hug

C'm'ere, you need to be goin'.

Gerry glares at Lanky, then dives back into the fray

All Munster, Munster, Munster, Munster.

The Lights change to an interior setting

Scene 10

We are in the Munster players' dressing-room

The crowd becomes the players — Tony Ward, Moss Keane, Donal Canniffe among them

Ward I thought we'd never get off the pitch.
Moss Keane The boss says we're to go out again, or we'll never get out of here. Oh, there's a phone call for you, Donal.
Canniffe It's probably the *Examiner* after an exclusive.
Moss Keane No, it's not the press. He said he was a friend of your brother's.

Backlighting comes up

Canniffe moves DR; *a spot comes up on him. He mimes using a telephone*

Canniffe No, this is Donal. ... Thanks. ..... No, go ahead. ... When? ... Yeah. ... Yeah. ... OK. ... Right. ... Thanks, Michael. (*He looks shocked by what he has heard*)

All the cast apart from Donal Canniffe gather at the back of the stage; they create the sound of the distant crowd by chanting "Munster Munster" in a stage whisper

Tony Ward moves to Donal Canniffe, oblivious to his news

Ward Donal, we're going back out.
Canniffe OK.
Ward Are you coming?
Canniffe Give me a minute, Tony; I'll follow you on.

The cheer gets wilder; the team has emerged

Donal listens to the cheer then walks off

Scene 11

The car park

Donal returns as Lanky and is joined by Marjorie, Spider, David and Sinbad the dog

David David.

A cold lighting state comes up C

Marjorie Marjorie.
Spider Spider.
Lanky Lanky.

Sinbad barks. He is glad to be out. He has gotten sick in the car

Spider It's not my fault he got sick all over the car, mister. You shouldn't have given him all them sausage rolls. My brother works in the bacon factory and you should see what they put into 'em; you'd never eat another sausage again.

There is a moment's pause while David and Marjorie survey the damage

   Mickeys an' everythin'.
Marjorie Pay the lad, David.

Spider is paid and goes

Marjorie There is no earthly way I am travelling to Cork in that car.

Lanky summons David

Lanky Let your wife off with the other pair. We'll drop your car and the dog at my place and let you come out on the tear with me.

Marjorie gives David and Lanky a sharp look

SCENE 12

Gerry Taxi!

A warm patch of lighting comes up C

Spider and Lanky, on all fours, form a taxi on the centre spot, Spider at the front, Lanky at the back. Sinbad the dog becomes the taxi driver who is about ninety

Gerry gets into the back of the taxi which is outside the ground. He's exhausted after struggling through the crowd

Gerry Bedford Row hospital, please.
Driver The baby place?
Gerry Yeah.
Driver Next to the Savoy.
Gerry Yeah.
Driver Let's see now, what'd be the quickest way?
Gerry Over Sarsfield bridge and up Henry Street.
Driver Oh, that'd do it right enough. I think we've missed most of the traffic.

Gerry is silent. The taxi driver tries to make conversation

Driver So, were you at the match ?
Gerry Ah, yeah.
Driver What was the score?
Gerry Twelve-nil.
Driver Oh, Munster didn't let themselves down too badly, so.
Gerry No, actually it was ... No.
Driver So are you visiting?
Gerry Yeah, my wife's expecting.
Driver When is she due?
Gerry About half an hour ago.
Driver I think I'd better put on my glasses. (*He does so, with great ceremony*)

The taxi accelerates to two hundred miles an hour. Gerry is pushed back in his seat. The taxi roars around corners, over potholes, then comes to a screeching halt

Driver Traffic.

Gerry is going to be sick. The taxi driver twiddles his fingers on the steering wheel, pushes his glasses up and looks around, then pushes his glasses back down again

   I think I can squeeze through there.
Gerry Noooo.

The taxi moves forward and goes up on two wheels as it squeezes through a gap; it takes a corner then goes down again

Driver Now just down the steps.

Gerry, the driver and the taxi actors nod their heads as the car goes down the steps

You know I think you'd nearly be as quick if you hopped out here.
Gerry Yeah! How much do I owe you?
Driver Ah, leave it. Buy the baby somethin' nice.
Gerry Bees.
Driver What ?
Gerry (*proudly*) Babies. She's havin' twins.
Driver (*after a quick admiring glance at Gerry's groin*) Good man yourself!

The Lights change to a warm, sombre interior

SCENE 13

Gerry becomes Seamus Dennisson; the taxi driver leaves with the Lanky actor

Seamus is joined by Tony Ward. Spider becomes Gerry McLoughlin and joins them too. They are downbeat

Seamus How did he hear?
McLoughlin Phone call.
Ward What happened?
McLoughlin Heart attack, in Cork during the game.
Seamus Poor Donal.
McLoughlin Pat Whelan will take over for him at the dinner.
Seamus Donal wouldn't want us mopin', lads, c'mon.

SCENE 14

Seamus leaves

Gerry McLoughlin becomes Spider, Tony Ward becomes Jasper

They are joined by Dandy and Ferret

Spider Spider.

The Lights change to a night-time exterior setting

Jasper Jasper.
Dandy Dandy.
Ferret Ferret.

Ferret addresses the audience

Ferret Word has got out. People are slinking away from the O'Mahonys bonfire in droves. Their ma is ragin'. She has six hundred Rice Krispie buns lined up next to one hundred paper cups and forty quart bottles of TK red lemonade. Well, TK or no TK, Limerick lads know bonfires. Our congregation gather, humbled, supplicant to the sight that greets them. They kneel, stand and crouch. They wait.

Spider comes c holding something aloft

Spider It is I, Spider, keeper of the burning oily rag on a broom handle.
Jasper
Dandy } *(together)* Aaah. *(They bow quickly to Spider)*
Ferret
Spider *(miming the following as he speaks)* The rag is placed on an old tray at the base of the tower. Its flame licks at other oily combustibles.

A red light comes up

All is fire.

The kids gaze in wonder at the huge fire. The stage is suffused with red light

SCENE 15

Jasper becomes David

Spider exits

During the following Dandy climbs on to Ferret's shoulders to become a huge New Zealand fan, Dandy's (the actress's) jersey covering Ferret's face

Lanky enters DL and joins David. They face the audience, masking Dandy and Ferret's transformation from the audience

Bridie enters and stands DC. She is a barmaid run off her feet

Lanky Two pints, please, Bridie.

The Lights change to an interior setting DS

David Do you have any Murphy's?

Bridie says something we don't hear

What?

Bridie speaks again

She says they've no glasses left, and if we want drink we have to find a pair of glasses.

Lanky Feckit, we've two chances of gettin' glasses out of this lot. We'll hare next door to Flannerry's and bring the pints in here for the crack.

Lanky and David turn their backs to the audience

Bridie Behind the bar Bridie Walsh is a blue-rinsed blur. Washing glasses. Pulling pints. "No glass, no drink!" is the catchcall for the evening. Gin and tonic? We've no more ice or lemon! Hot port? The kettle's blown up. Four Guinness, three Smithwicks, a vodka and coke and a Black Bush: six pounds, seventy-six new pence, please. (*To Lanky*) Yes, sir, what can I get for you?

Lanky and David turn back

Lanky Two Murphy's, Bridie. You'd want to give them glasses a good wash, Bridie; I found them in the lane.
Bridie Sure, what harm? 'Tis clean dirt.

The huge New Zealand fan appears at the bar

(*Looking up*) Yes, sir!

The Ferret actor, his face hidden by the actress's jersey, speaks in a booming voice; the actress mouths the words

New Zealand Fan A pint of Guinness.
Bridie Yes, sir!
Lanky C'm'ere, cheer up, you can't win them all.
David Yes, Lanky's right, enjoy yourself.
New Zealand Fan What do they call you?
Lanky Lanky.
New Zealand Fan Why?
Lanky (*looking up at him*) 'Cause I'm so tall.

The Lights change to an interior setting covering the whole stage

Scene 16

They become the Munster players; Bridie becomes Seamus Dennisson, David becomes Tony Ward, the top of the New Zealand Fan gets down and becomes Moss Keane

Seamus What are we waiting for lads? I'm starving.

Tucker Their royal highnesses the All Blacks have something planned. Tom Kiernan says we're to take our seats. They're going to perform some sort of Maori battle tribute.

Moss Keane Go way!

Ward Yeah, the Maoris used to do it after a battle to salute the tribe that beat them.

Moss Keane What's it like?

Ward I don't know, but they don't look too happy.

The Lights change to a spooky backlight

They all become the All Blacks as Maoris in a weird Haka stance. They dramatically rip out their hearts and watch them beat in their hands in unison. Then they throw the hearts on the ground, stamp on them and display the result to the enemy. They then slowly raise their hands to their hearts

All Blacks Hi.

They raise their hands over their heads

Hoo.

Beat. They collapse on their knees and march dwarf-like to the front of the stage, singing an adult version of the Seven Dwarfs' song

Robertson We salute the great Munster team.

All Blacks (*in ascending notes*) Eam, eam, eam!

Robertson We are not worthy to sniff your steam.

All Blacks Steam, steam, steam. Heee!

The Lights change to an interior setting

There is a big cheer from all the cast

Pat Whelan calls them to order

Whelan As you know I'm filling in tonight for Donal Canniffe whose father died this afternoon in Cork during the game. Dan Canniffe was a great sportsman in his day and I would like to begin the evening's proceedings with a minute's silence in his honour.

There follows a five second silence

Scene 17

We're back in the bar. There are a bunch of Munster fans — Lanky and David among them

Lanky One singer, one song.

The interior lighting brightens

Crowd Come on, David.
David Ah, no, no, no no.
Lanky Jesus, David, you're bending my ear all night with your Musical Society antics.
David But I don't know what to sing!
Lanky Anything. You start singing and we'll all join in.
David (*singing*) "I don't know how to love him …"

One of the fans becomes Spider

Spider Scatter!

The Lights change to a night-time exterior setting, with the effect of a fire

Everyone, except David, hits the deck

David (*bewildered*) What is it?
Spider Mossy fucked a load of t'ree-o-t'ree bullets into the bonfire.

David becomes Jasper

Jasper Jesus. Where did he get them?
Spider Robbed 'em above from the FCA.

There are several loud explosions. The kids think it is safe to get up; they stand. Another series of explosions sends them diving for cover again. This happens three times

Jasper Is anybody hurted?
Spider Don't be stupid, sur' the FCA never hit fuck all!

The Lights change to an interior setting

Jasper and Spider leave

SCENE 18

The others get up

Wilson supports Mary at a 60° angle with his hands in the middle of her back; she is in a hospital bed. Lanky becomes a nurse caring for Mary

Gerry enters

The Nurse looks at Gerry disapprovingly. Gerry is mortified but persists. The Nurse wakes Mary. They look at Gerry together. Gerry indicates that he wants the Nurse to leave

Nurse (*whispering*) I'll just be outside if you need me Mary, OK? (*She gives Gerry one last dirty look*)

The Nurse finally leaves

Gerry Did I miss it?
Mary Yeah. Two boys!

Silence

Do you want to see them?
Gerry God, yeah.

The babies (played by the David and Spider actors) come on

And you're sure they're boys?

The babies look at one another

What about the names?
Mary Munster won?
Gerry Yeah.
Mary Good game?

Gerry Yeah, Mary. What about the names?
Mary Oh, don't worry, I have the names.

The Lights change to a night-time exterior setting, with the effect of a fire

SCENE 19

The babies become Spider and Monica

Everyone else returns to the benches

Spider throws something on to the bonfire and delightedly watches it burn. Monica observes him

Monica Hallo, Spider.
Spider What are you doing here? This is a boys-only bonfire.
Monica I'm Monica.
Spider I know who you are. You're Pat O'Mahony's little sister. You got Ferret thrown out of the Scouts.

Pause. They look at each other

Monica I've come to see your big fire.

They both look at the fire

Spider Well, you've seen it, now feck off.
Monica How old are you?
Spider Fourteen.
Monica Are not.
Spider Well, thirteen.

Monica makes her way across the stage to Spider. She is inches from him. Close enough to kiss

Monica You did a good job, Spider.

They look at the fire. Monica plucks up her courage and kisses Spider. Spider is stunned

Monica exits, skipping

Ferret enters

Ferret Spider, Weasel is here from O'Mahony's. He's got chips! Spider ?
Spider Yeah, comin'.

The fire effect dies

Scene 20

Ferret and Spider go on all fours C, making a platform

Tony Ward and Seamus Dennisson come forward

Seamus What are you doing out here on the pitch, Tony ?
Ward Just one last look, Seamus. We beat the All Blacks twelve-nil!

Scene 21

Seamus moves to the platform made by the Ferret and Spider actors at the beginning of the previous scene. The Lights change to a sombre interior setting

Seamus lies on the platform. He is now the corpse of Dan Canniffe. The actress enters; she and the Tony Ward actor support Dan's head and feet

There is a moment's pause to let this settle

Donal enters. He kisses his father's face and looks at the body

Canniffe It was a great game, Dad. You would have been proud of us. We must have had Mick Mackey's hurley in the ground. Thanks for everything.

Donal blesses himself and returns to the benches

Scene 22

The scene returns to the pub

Dan Canniffe becomes Gerry, Donal Canniffe returns as Lanky; David and three others make up the party. The others have been listening to David sing for half an hour and are exhausted and bored

The Lights come up brightly. David sings the last line of "I Don't Know How To Love Him"

The others cheer the song anyway

Lanky Ladies and gentlemen, today is an historic day. Not only have brave Munster defeated the All Blacks, but our friend and fellow loyal supporter of Shannon Rugby Club, Gerry ——
David Up Shannon!
Crowd (*puzzled*) Up Shannon!
Lanky — has become a father. In years to come people will ask you where were you on this day ...
Gerry (*joining the others at the bar*) Two boys, two boys, six and seven pounds.

Lanky hands Gerry a pint

Crowd Gerry ——
Lanky (*raising a toast*) To Gerry and Mary.
Crowd To Gerry and Mary.

They drink

Lanky So, Gerry. What about the names?
Crowd Yeah, Gerry. What about the names?

Long beat

Gerry Gary and Owen.

The crowd is shocked, especially Lanky

David (*laughing uncontrollably*) Oh, that's very good.

The crowd looks menacingly at David

Gary Owen is the ... (*He thinks better of completing this line*)

The crowd looks at Gerry again

Gerry They'll make two fine props for Munster!

Lanky is disgusted. Gerry looks around for support but none is forthcoming

(*To Lanky; singing*) There is an isle
A bonny isle
Stands proudly from

The crowd reluctantly joins in

Crowd   Stands proudly from the sea
Gerry   And dearer far
                  In all this world
                  Is that dear isle
Lanky   Is that dear isle to me.
Gerry ⎫
Lanky ⎭ It is not that alone it stands
Crowd Alone it stands
Gerry ⎫
Lanky ⎭ While all around is fresh and fair
Crowd Is fresh and fair
All But because it is my native land

The Lights get even brighter

   And my home, my home is there.

The crowd lifts Gerry shoulder high

   (*Shouting*) Munster!

Black-out

Frankie Flynn's version of "There is an isle" plays over the curtain call

FURNITURE AND PROPERTY LIST

ACT I and ACT II

On stage: Judo mats — black or green with white tape around the edge
Benches

LIGHTING PLOT

ACT I

To open: Darkness

Cue 1	The actors stand in Haka formation *Bring up backlighting*	(Page 1)
Cue 2	**Wilson** lands facing US *Bring up spot C*	(Page 1)
Cue 3	**Gerry** is shouldered off *Bring up full lighting*	(Page 1)
Cue 4	All but **Wilson** groan *Change to cold night-time exterior*	(Page 2)
Cue 5	**Fox**: "Bite, boot and bollock." *Snap to bright daytime exterior*	(Page 3)
Cue 6	**Gerry**: "I'm telling you, every turn I make." *Change to night-time exterior*	(Page 4)
Cue 7	**Spider**: "Spider." *Snap to bright daytime exterior*	(Page 6)
Cue 8	**Robertson**: Yeah. *Snap to night-time exterior with white floodlight effect*	(Page 9)
Cue 9	**Russ**: " … will personally deflower you myself." *Snap off white floodlights*	(Page 10)
Cue 10	**Seamus**: " … no matter who I hit." *Snap on white floodlights*	(Page 11)
Cue 11	**Russ**: " … till after the game on Tuesday." *Change to interior*	(Page 11)
Cue 12	**Kiernan**: " … make the first tackle count." *Change to cold interior*	(Page 12)

Cue 13	**Donal Canniffe** moves DR, **Dan** DL	(Page 14)
	Bring up spots DR *and* DL	
Cue 14	**Canniffe**: "Thanks, Dad, see you soon."	(Page 14)
	Snap off spot on **Canniffe**	
Cue 15	**Dan**: "Good luck, son."	(Page 15)
	Fade spot on **Dan**; *bring up interior with orange glow*	
Cue 16	**Kiernan**: "Stu Wilson."	(Page 15)
	Bring up spot UC	
Cue 17	**Kiernan** turns off the video	(Page 16)
	Cut orange glow	
Cue 18	**Kiernan** flicks on the lights	(Page 16)
	Brighten interior	
Cue 19	The cast faces the audience, growling. Then freeze	(Page 16)
	Strange version of orange interior	
Cue 20	**All** (*singing*) "… Have I any fault to find."	(Page 17)
	Cross-fade to normal interior DR	
Cue 21	**Haden**: "It could get messy, mate."	(Page 17)
	Bring up spot on **The Girl with the Harp**	
Cue 22	**The Girl with the Harp**: " … *se marbh ansin*."	(Page 18)
	Change to daytime exterior	
Cue 23	**Marjorie**: " I think you'd better pay the lad, David."	(Page 19)
	Change to night-time exterior	
Cue 24	**Lanky**: "Well, it gave me an idea."	(Page 20)
	Change to dark interior	
Cue 25	**Lanky**: "OK."	(Page 21)
	Change to night-time exterior	
Cue 26	**Gerry** pants	(Page 22)
	Change to spooky setting	
Cue 27	**Mourie**: "Kia mo."	(Page 22)
	Change to different spooky setting	
Cue 28	**Mourie**: "Ringia packia."	(Page 22)
	Bring up full white lighting	

Cue 29	**Gerry**: "Come on, Munster." *Change to bright cold exterior with spot* DR	(Page 22)
Cue 30	**BBC Commentator**: " ... the clear blue Munster sky." *Cut* DR *spot*	(Page 22)
Cue 31	Four actors form a scrum *Floor-level lighting on scrum with warm fill from above*	(Page 23)
Cue 32	**All**: "Line out." *Change to cold exterior*	(Page 24)
Cue 33	**Ashworth**: " ... you savage." *Brighten lights*	(Page 25)
Cue 34	**Kiernan**: " ... the blindside at speed." *Bring up lights very brightly*	(Page 26)
Cue 35	**Seamus**: "Ahhhhhhh." *Backlighting on scrum*	(Page 27)
Cue 36	**Lanky**: "Jesus, he's killed him." *Change to cold exterior*	(Page 27)
Cue 37	**Seamus**: "Well, they won't try that again in a hurry." *Bring up weird orange interior*	(Page 27)
Cue 38	All return to being players *Return to cold exterior*	(Page 28)
Cue 39	**Brendan Foley** moves L *Bring up spot* DR	(Page 28)
Cue 40	**Gerry**: " ... keep it tight, boy." *Cut* DR *spot*	(Page 28)
Cue 41	**Ward**: "Good easy ball into my chest." *Bring up spot* L *on* **Ward** *and* **Kiernan**	(Page 28)
Cue 42	**Kiernan**: " ... all the better." *Cut spot* L	(Page 28)
Cue 43	**Bowen**: "Jim Bowen rushes on to it." *Bring up spot on* **Gerry** DR	(Page 29)
Cue 44	**Gerry**: "... If he collects it he's through." *Bring up spot* C	(Page 29)

ACT II

Cue 59   **All**: "Half-time."   (Page 39)
              Bring up cold exterior

Cue 60   **David** becomes **Ward**   (Page 40)
              Bring up spot tight on **Ward**'s face

Cue 61   **Ward**: " ... is Donal's voice ..."   (Page 40)
              Cut spot

Cue 62   **Canniffe**: "We are forty minutes from history, lads."   (Page 40)
              Bring up spot on **Ward**

Cue 63   **Ward**: " ... something is happening."   (Page 40)
              Bring up spot DR; *dim lights on* DL *quarter of stage*

Cue 64   **BBC Commentator**: " ... with his friends in Cork City." (Page 41)
              Bring up lights DL

Cue 65   All fall into a pile UR   (Page 41)
              Change to cold exterior

Cue 66   **Mourie**: "Dive in."   (Page 42)
              Change to warm UR

Cue 67   **Mourie**: " Protect. Ball. Break."   (Page 43)
              Bring up cold exterior UL

Cue 68   **Tucker**: "Break!"   (Page 43)
              Cross-fade to warm interior DR

Cue 69   **Dan**: " ... there'll be some row."   (Page 44)
              Bring up spot DR

Cue 70   **BBC Commentator**: "Munster breathe again."   (Page 44)
              Return to cold exterior

Cue 71   **Lanky** makes his way DR   (Page 45)
              Bring up spot on **Lanky** DR

Cue 72   **BBC Commentator**: "Munster, Munster."   (Page 46)
              Bring up cold lighting on crowd

Cue 73   **BBC Commentator** retracts the microphone   (Page 46)
              Fade lights on crowd

Cue 74   **BBC Commentator**: "The crowd love it."   (Page 46)
              Return to cold exterior; cut spot

Cue 91	**Moss Keane**: " … a friend of your brother's." *Backlighting comes up*	(Page 57)
Cue 92	**Canniffe** moves DR *Bring spot up DR*	(Page 57)
Cue 93	**David**: "David." *Bring up cold lighting* C	(Page 58)
Cue 94	**Gerry**: "Taxi!" *Bring up warm patch* C	(Page 58)
Cue 95	**Driver**: "Good man yourself!" *Change to warm, sombre interior*	(Page 60)
Cue 96	**Spider**: "Spider." *Change to night-time exterior*	(Page 60)
Cue 97	**Spider**: " … other oily combustibles." *Bring up red light*	(Page 61)
Cue 98	Kids gaze in wonder at fire *Intensify red light*	(Page 61)
Cue 99	**Lanky**: "Two pints, please, Bridie." *Change to interior* DS	(Page 61)
Cue 100	**Lanky**: "'Cause I'm so tall." *Change to interior over whole stage*	(Page 62)
Cue 101	**Ward**: " … but they don't look too happy." *Spooky backlight*	(Page 63)
Cue 102	**All Blacks**: "Steam, steam, steam. Heee!" *Change to interior*	(Page 63)
Cue 103	**Lanky**: "One singer, one song." *Brighten interior lighting*	(Page 64)
Cue 104	**Spider**: "Scatter!" *Change to night-time exterior with fire effect*	(Page 64)
Cue 105	**Spider**: " … never hit fuck all!" *Change to interior*	(Page 65)
Cue 106	**Mary**: " … I have the names." *Change to night-time exterior with fire effect*	(Page 66)

Cue 107   **Spider**: "Yeah, comin'."   (Page 67)
           Fire effect dies

Cue 108   **Seamus** moves to the platform   (Page 67)
           Change to sombre interior

Cue 109   To open SCENE 22. When ready   (Page 67)
           Bring up bright interior

Cue 110   **All**: "But because it is my native land."   (Page 69)
           Brighten lights even more

Cue 111   **All**: "Munster!"   (Page 69)
           Black-out

EFFECTS PLOT

ACT I

Cue 1	As play begins *Drums*	(Page 1)
Cue 2	**Graham** tries to punch **Canniffe** *Whistle blows*	(Page 32)
Cue 3	Black-out *Music: "Staying Alive"*	(Page 38)

ACT II

Cue 4	The actors take up their positions *Drums followed by baby scream*	(Page 39)
Cue 5	**Spider**: "Robbed 'em above from the FCA." *Several loud explosions; four series in all*	(Page 64)
Cue 6	Black-out *Music: Frankie Flynn's "There is an isle"*	(Page 69)